HOW TO FLIP A HOUSE

7 Fundamentals Of A Highly Successful Flip

Brant Phillips

THIS BOOK IS DEDICATED TO:
My beautiful wife and three wonderful children...
You are everything to me

And to all those seeking financial freedom
and all the best that life has to offer, I am with you

ACKNOWLEDGEMENTS

To have success in real estate investing means having a trustworthy and dependable TEAM. The people you surround yourself with are literally the difference between success and failure. I have been extremely fortunate to be surrounded by a group of people that have helped me to achieve great success and I would like to take this opportunity to introduce them to you and let you know how they have helped me along:

First and foremost, my loving wife Tara. She has supported me in my entrepreneurial pursuits when we were dead broke and continues to support me today. She is a constant source of encouragement with her strong faith and love.

Jack Mize, Real estate mentor and internet marketing Genius, showed me the ropes of how to double my cash-flow with affordable housing and many techniques for making 'fast nickels over slow dimes' and all the while getting 'cash back at closing'.

Mindy, my personal assistant, you couldn't have come along at a better time. Your addition to the company has allowed me to expand to bigger horizons...I now even have time to write a book!

Chris Adkins, the 'young Prime' to be. You're the apprentice that helps keep my wheels turning and won't let me rest on my laurels. I'm looking forward to the millions that are to come very, very soon.

Manesh Hardeo, Networth Realty, who brought me my very first real estate deal when I was extremely 'wet behind the ears' and he's brought me dozens of houses since...thanks for all of your help (and patience) in the beginning and, more importantly thanks for keeping the deals coming to me!

And to everyone else that has helped me along the way, family members and friends, mentors and the many great trailblazers before me who were kind enough to leave "Maps" (in the form of mentoring and books) to show others that success can be duplicated. I am truly grateful to each and every one of you that have helped me along the way. You are appreciated.

CONTENTS

INTRODUCTION: THE JOURNEY BEGINS HERE

Buying, renovating (or more commonly referred to as 'rehabbing') and selling a house for profit, known as House Flipping, is one of the most exciting ways to make money in Real Estate.

There are potentially huge paydays awaiting you if you do this the right way.

I've personally made over $60,000 in a 2 month period on a single flip. In fact, during the week I was writing this book, I sold 3 deals in a 90 day period for a combined profit of over $100,000 and did another deal recently that made over $100,000 net in only 5 months.

You too can experience the same success if you follow the proven Flipping Principles experienced investors use. However, if you choose to veer away from proven systems that work, and decide to learn the business by yourself, you must beware - great financial loss can occur.

So take this hint: Don't go *there*, just follow me and you'll do just fine.

I often wonder, what makes flipping houses so wildly popular? Maybe it's the satisfaction an investor gets from taking an old beat up home, rehabbing it and turning it into the most beautiful house on the block. Maybe it's the excitement portrayed by all those real estate TV shows and infomercials that became quite the fad a few years ago. Maybe it's the possibility of making piles of money in relatively short periods of time.

Speaking for myself, the strongest motivation for me is the pursuit of achieving financial freedom and wealth through real estate investing while at the same time doing something I'm truly passionate about and working with people that I enjoy doing business with.

While I'm quite certain that making large sums of cash appeals to a lot of people, hopefully, that's not the only reason you're reading this book and contemplating on the possibility of taking on the challenge of successfully flipping houses.

You see, flipping a house involves much more than simply trying to make money. This process can be a complete emotional, physical and even psychological, roller coaster at times. Flipping houses is kind of like a mixture of Fox News and MTV, or better yet, Wall Street and Las Vegas.

In other words, it's a well blended mixture of analytical due diligence and entrepreneurial *dice rolling* as you decide to 'take a chance' when the numbers look good.

I think you get the picture. :-)

It is definitely true that there's great satisfaction and pride once you make the commitment of purchasing a distressed property that has been neglected for years, work on getting the house cleaned up and rehabbed, and finally transforming it into a home - all while trying to stay within an acceptable budget and time frame that can leave you plenty of space to make a profit. All these elements combine into one action packed chain of events that can truly be life changing - all the while helping to improve the community as well.

And, yeah, I get it, if you do it right, the money's not too bad either! :-)

So come along with me as we go through what I've identified, based on my own extensive experience flipping houses and making huge paydays, as the **7 Fundamentals of a Highly Successful Flip**.

We'll cover a huge area of the real estate game that's going to be crucial to your success.

My goal is that by the end of this book, you will have gained the right motivation and mindset combined with the proper knowledge and skillsets needed to be able to execute the 7 Fundamentals of Flipping to your own business and begin creating your own wealth and cash by flipping houses.

Let's get started.

CHAPTER ONE

WHO IS BRANT & WHY YOU SHOULD READ THIS BOOK

My name is Brant Phillips and, in many ways, I'm a lot like you.

Like a lot of people, while chasing the *American Dream* and in my personal *Pursuit of Happiness*, my goal to succeed always seemed to evade my grasp.

I wanted to provide a better life for my family and rise to great heights like many others have done before me.

However, as time went by, I found myself just barely getting by and struggling to make ends meet working a job that I did not enjoy (to say the least) and seeing my dream slip further and further away.

Not too long ago, I was serving as a Police Officer in Houston, Texas. I really enjoyed being in law enforcement for many years while I was single and working long hours, weekends and holidays was no big deal. But after I got married and my wife and I had our first child, the long hours I had to work left no time to be with my family.

Like a lot of others, I worked double shifts, night shifts, weekends and holidays. You name it and I would do it. I did it because I knew that's what it takes to provide for my family.

Unfortunately, it didn't take long before my career in law enforcement began to put a huge strain on my marriage and my family environment.

Not wanting to sacrifice family, I decided to pursue another career path in my quest to provide a better future for our family.

After almost seven years in law enforcement, I turned in my badge and convinced myself that the 'grass would be greener' on the other side.

I decided to try my hand in corporate America.

After only my first year trying to climb the corporate ladder, I began to feel the exact same way again - I felt overworked, underpaid and with very little time for my family. I realized, in a short period of time, I had turned into a rat caught in the never-ending race that is corporate America.

During that period, my wife and I were expecting our second child. This new and added responsibility, coupled with the ever-present thought of being stuck in the corporate grind for another 25-30 years began to eat away at me.

It was a rather depressing thought. I kept thinking there had to be another way - a better way.

However, I wasn't sure which direction to go to get out of my situation. I was confused and a feeling of growing helplessness was beginning to tighten its grip around me.

All I knew was there's a voice inside of me that was refusing to give up.

It was my life's turning point.

I decided to avert my attention from the growing fit of desperation and just concentrate on that voice that urged me to move forward.

It was then that I found the determination to find the BETTER WAY.

"When the student is ready, the teacher will appear"

-Ancient Proverb

By sheer luck, or fate, or whatever you want to call it, I happened to meet a guy at a social function I attended with my wife.

I think he and I were both standing by a punch bowl waiting for our wives to return or something like that. We started talking and somehow, our normal small talk and chit chat kind of stuff turned to real estate (at that time, I had ZERO knowledge about real estate).

As it turned out, the guy had been in real estate for years and from the sounds of it, made millions investing in real estate over the years. He said he was around my age (I was in my early 30's then) when he began buying and fixing up houses, which he either flipped or rented out. He told me he eventually progressed into doing bigger projects such as apartment complexes and commercial buildings. Then he told me about a project he had recently completed that profited him over $1 million dollars!

I was really hooked then.

He told me the first step he took, when he finally decided to buy his first investment property years ago, was to make a personal commitment to take back control of his life. I asked him what he meant by that and he told me about the job he used to have which basically monopolized every waking moment he had, controlled his time, sucked every bit of his energy, and yet, still managed to leave him broke as a joke.

He said that what practically led him to real estate investing was a firm desire he built inside of him to find a better way to provide a bright future for his family, other than keep himself trapped in a grueling job for the rest of his life - a job that took everything he had to offer and barely gave him enough to make ends meet. He was tired of allowing the financial freedom and security of himself and his family be controlled and dictated by other the people - the people for whom he worked his butt off, yet wouldn't even spare a minute to fire him if need be.

I marveled at how similar our life stories were.

He also impressed upon me the importance of having a "Financial Education". He explained this meant having a clear understanding on WHY the rich kept getting richer.

He also told me that approximately 70% of wealthy Americans built their fortunes through real estate.

It was as if the proverbial light bulb lit up in my head! I knew, at that moment, I was going to commit myself to learning how to invest in real estate. There was no doubt at this time.

I still remember his parting words for me that night, *"If you want to experience the best that life has to offer, you have to take control of your own destiny."*

WEALTH TIP:

TAKE CONTROL OF YOUR DESTINY

Obviously, it was one of the most meaningful conversations to ever occur in my life. It was exactly what I needed to hear to get started.

Problem was, apart from knowing for certain real estate investing was my ticket out of my misery, I didn't have a concrete idea on how to get started.

Realizing I was treading on uncharted waters, I began with the obvious - *get familiar with the subject*. I began reading every real estate book I could get my hands on. I read everything about real estate investing like my life depended on it - and in a way, it really did. I was relentless!

I can't emphasize this enough: There's no such thing as "over-reading" on a subject that can affect your financial future and freedom. The more you know about a task, project or undertaking, the better you will become at accomplishing it. And so I read and read and read. And after I got tired of reading, I took a break by reading some more. :)

You see I was at a point in my life where I was utterly disgruntled about the state of my financial situation. I was completely frustrated and tired of being broke and working a job that I didn't like.

I knew I had to do something. Deep down inside, I knew I could figure out a way to *create* a better life for my family. And even if I didn't know the exact specific first steps I should take, I knew if I could just focus enough at knowing and mastering everything I could about real estate investing, finding the first steps wouldn't be such a problem at all.

"The best way to predict the future is to create it"

-Abraham Lincoln

Like I said, I began to read everything and anything I thought could help me get to where I wanted to go. I was so stoked the more I read on the subject, the more I hungered to know more.

I can't emphasize it enough: THE MORE YOU READ THE MORE YOU WILL GROW.

I can't help but feel bad when people say they don't have the time to read. I believe it's just a matter of motivation. Let me ask you, what if you knew for certain you would become a millionaire if you read at least three books a week? Would you still say you don't have time to read?

The first thing I always ask people if they say they don't have enough time to read is, "How much time do you spend watching TV?"

Did you know the average American spends 4 hours each day watching TV? According to the A.C. Nielsen Co., that's the amount they have reported, 4 hours per day. That translates to 28 hours per week, or 2 months of non-stop TV-watching per year!

If you're like the average American watching 4 hours per week, if you were to focus that time into reading, you could probably read 4 or 5 books per week. Need I ask which activity is directly proportional to a person's success?

I (like many of the successful people I've met) watch very little television. And when I do watch it, (mainly football, Shark Tank and a little bit of the news) I record it so I can fast forward through all of the commercials and time waster stuff. I can watch a typical three hour plus NFL football game in a about an hour and not miss a single play!

Besides, with technology these days, you can take advantage of audio books and listen while doing other things like driving, exercising or whatever. When I'm driving, I am almost always listening to audio books. You can easily listen to an audio book a week while you're exercising, working, or whatever. You can even download these to your phone or MP3 player and listen with your earphones.

So really, there's practically no excuse for you not to be continually educating yourself with the help of presently existing technologies and good old time management.

Let me remind you though, not just to read books about real estate investing or books on making money. You don't want to become some lopsided or a one-track minded person. You need to be well rounded in all aspects of your life.

Think about it, what's the point in making mountains of money if you have no higher purpose in life? Even worse, what's the use of acquiring massive wealth if it does not equate to having more happiness and peace in your life?

Yes, I do read a lot of business and real estate books because I enjoy making money, but I also read a lot of motivational/self-help books, health/fitness and even faith based, spiritual books.

Now I know what you're reading right now isn't exactly a time management or motivational book. That doesn't mean, though, that I shouldn't drive home the fact that if you're not committed to furthering your education, then you're most likely not going to make it in this business or any other entrepreneurial pursuit.

If you want to succeed, YOU HAVE TO READ.

It's not optional.

SO DO IT!

WEALTH TIP:

READ RELENTLESSLY

Another thing I did when I was getting started was to seek out mentors to help me speed up the learning curve.

Effective mentorship is the fastest and most efficient way to achieve success when you are first starting out.

I found my first mentors by getting plugged into real estate 'circles' (This is also a good practice in order to develop a great working network for yourself as real estate circles or local REIA's (Real Estate Investment Association) are an excellent way to meet contractors, property managers, sellers, buyers, private lenders, Realtors and other people and professionals you'll need when building a successful team. More of that to come later.

There are 2 types of mentoring. There are mentors who are willing to show you some ropes for free, or let you do some work for them and 'trade' your hustle/efforts for some of their advice and experience. And there are paid mentors and coaches.

I've heard some people complain about having to pay someone to provide mentorship. I'm telling you, don't be too tight in this area because with the right coaching and mentoring, you can drastically speed up your results and avoid some of the pitfalls along the way.

The opportunity to get inside the head of a person who's actually achieved the kind of success you are aspiring for is one of the greatest ways to learn. There's nothing more costly in business than to try to learn something yourself at the risk of time, capital and effort, when you can actually skip the learning curve and just follow the advice of someone who's actually been there, seen that and done that.

Besides, if you do a good job of choosing an effective mentor, you can take action on what they tell you to do, you'll make that money you paid for mentorship back in a short period of time. If not, then you may not have found the right mentor, or perhaps you're not doing the work.

I'm talking not just out of my own experience, but also that of countless other successful entrepreneurs who can attest that while experience is the best teacher, you don't necessarily have to be the one to experience failure in order to learn from it.

I give a ton of credit to my mentors because they have been fundamental to the success I've achieved. I am forever grateful I have found mentors who were willing to go out of their way to help me out and show me all the specific steps I needed to take in order to fast track my own journey towards financial freedom.

At present, I'm a part of a several mastermind groups. A **Mastermind Group** is a group of like-minded individuals (in this case, individuals focused on achieving success in their respective fields) who come together on a regular basis to help support each other to grow in their respective endeavors. It's like a group of mentors mentoring each other.

I pay big bucks to be a part of some of these groups and many of them aren't even located in my own city. I have to drive four hours to get to one of the Mastermind Meetings every month. The others, we use GoToMeeting and Facetime type software, so we can meet via computer. But I'm telling you, the resulting business growth from my mastermind meetings is worth every dollar I pay for it.

The returns I've received on those financial and time investments have been huge to say the least, and I would gladly pay double to keep going to some of them (Just don't tell my mentors! LOL!)

I also joined a couple of local real estate investing clubs to help, not just in my personal education within the world of real estate investing, but more to develop a network of professionals I can work with when doing deals.

This is also a MUST DO for anyone who wants to be successful in this business.

I can't stress enough how important it is to be active in your local real estate investment clubs. Most of my 'team' has been established through various contacts that began in investment and networking clubs.

Furthermore, real estate markets, cycles, laws, regulations, etc. are constantly evolving and changing. You have to stay up to date on the changes that are taking place in your local market or you're going to get left behind. That's another benefit of attending your local REIA meetings because they frequently have industry experts provide legal and market updates that are crucial to your business.

I ADMIT IT

I am what many call a "Type A" personality.

This means I often take aggressive action and sometimes throw caution to the wind.

Holding true to form, only a couple of months after I started reading books about real estate, I made a decision to start buying 'fixer upper' houses.

At the time, my wife and I were still living in an apartment and we had NO MONEY in the bank.

I still remember, one night when my wife and I decided to add up our net worth. We came up with a number that's very unflattering to say the least: Zero.

Zero Cash + No Assets = Broke!

We both had decent credit scores, but we had NO CASH to put down on a home. We still hadn't been married very long and we had just finished paying off our student loans, credit cards, wedding stuff, etc. and we were tapped out.

If you've ever heard the "rags to riches" stories of people starting with nothing and being able to buy homes using none of their own cash or credit…

…Well, I'm telling you, it's true, I am living proof of it.

In fact, during my first year as an investor, I ended up buying 10 houses all while working a full-time job, using zero cash and while living in that apartment and working my full-time job.

Looking back on it, I find it amusing that I was buying and investing in real estate while living in an apartment. We did eventually buy a home and have since upgraded to our dream home, but I was so focused on my goals, that there wasn't a whole lot of time to think about moving or looking for a personal home.

Since the time I started, I have purchased close to 50 rental properties, with equity I am keeping for long-term cash flow.

Nowadays however, I'm more focused on being a "House Flipper." That's my real estate passion so to speak.

In the printed version of my book, I display a few of my recent closing statements to help readers understand why I consider this a true passion and provide proof of the deals that I've done.

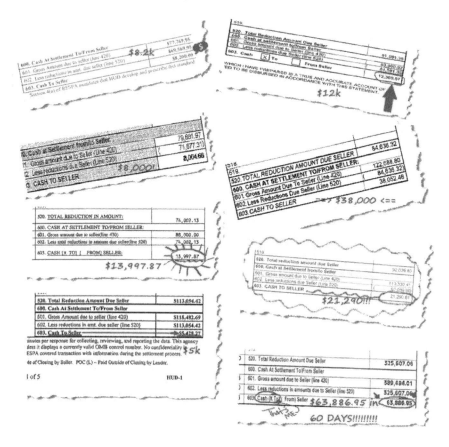

One of the closing statements was a wire to my bank account for $63,886.95, which was more than what I made the previous year working a job. Cool, huh? :-)

Please understand I'm not showing these closing statements to brag or impress anyone. What I am trying to do is impress upon you of what's possible when you execute a profitable flip and build a successful real estate investing business. Yes, you can experience these types of results too.

Remember, when I got started investing in real estate, I was working long hours at a full-time job while raising a family and I was broke as a joke. Back then, my wife and I struggled to raise enough money to pay the bills and still have enough left to raise our 2-year old son. But now, with the help of real estate investing, my family is living comfortably, we now have 4 kids and I can say I'm very proud of the life that my wife and I are able to provide for our family.

More than the financial wealth real estate investing has helped me achieve, what's even more important is the knowledge that this financial freedom allows me to become a better father, better husband and better person - while increasing our wealth.

Not bad for a former cop, eh? :-)

So, how was I able to buy my first investment property when I had zero cash? Believe it or not, I actually borrowed money on a credit card to put money down on the first house I bought. For the record, buying houses on a credit card is NOT something I recommend. It's very, very risky and if you don't end up with a good deal that makes you enough money, you can end up with a pretty sticky situation that's very difficult to get unstuck from. But during that time, I didn't know better and doing it seemed to be the only course I had if I was really serious about becoming an investor.

Everything worked out, so I don't regret that decision one bit. But let me just be clear, I don't recommend anyone buying an investment property on a credit card unless you know very well what you're doing.

After closing that first investment property, I have gone on to rehab over 500 homes for myself and many of my clients through my investment property construction business. We average somewhere around 50 investment property rehabs a year.

I now have a whole staff handling most of the heavy lifting in the business. We've grown to the point where we have a full time project manager, salesperson and admin staff. We even use several VA's (Virtual Assistants) to help us out in the business as well.

Presently, in addition to pursuing my own investments and flip deals and running my company, Invest Home Pro, a lot of my focus is spent working with investors on how to strategize their investment deals, how to manage and plan deals for maximum profitability, raising capital, etc. I do some of the coaching on a 1-on-1 setting and I also run a coaching program for Men called, Breakthrough At The Beach. It's a mix between Business/Real Estate and some of the personal development training I've been through that teaches Men not only how to create a thriving Investment Business, but also some of the tools needed to create the ideal life along the way in some of the other core areas. It's a long way from my former work as a cop and I'm loving every moment of it.

I'm telling you, there's nothing like finding your passion in life.

When you are able to do something you really like and really enjoy, and you get paid to do it, life becomes so much more enjoyable.

I really want to encourage you to pursue what you are passionate about in life and learn to monetize it. You'll find that your whole future is going to start looking very, very sweet indeed. And if this passion happens to be flipping houses and investing in real estate, then you'll have opportunities as well to help other people on their journey, and that's very rewarding as well.

Basically, the point I'm driving at is this: Flipping houses is one of the few ways you can get started with ZERO knowledge, ZERO experience or even ZERO money and still find a way to achieve financial success and freedom from a J.O.B.

I did it. And you can too.

Nowadays, I'm being asked to go on the news, hosting seminars, running my company www.InvestHomePro.com, coaching other real estate investors and I'm even being considered to star in one of those "Flipping Houses" TV shows.

Just so you know, I'm going to periodically reference Internet sites and information in this book, so when you have a chance, you can reference them here: www.FlipAHouseBook.com/resources.

So be sure to check out the resources page if you want to watch me being interviewed on the news, my television show pilot and some event highlights on the resources page.

Some days, I feel like I'm living a dream.

Since I started flipping houses I have been able to quit my job, increase my income, experience more freedom and pursue many different things I'm passionate about. I'm not going to lie – quitting my job was one of the greatest and scariest moments in my life at the time. But now looking back, it was a defining moment for me and has been an incredible journey.

With everything I have achieved so far, the least I can do is to share with others what I have learned, hence, this book.

I want to help you achieve the similar success that I have experienced. All you need to do is believe and commit to applying the things I will share with you in this book.

I am a sucker for the underdog stories of people defying odds and achieving success. It's one of the reasons I wrote this book.

I do have one favor to ask. If you use the Fundamentals in this book to go out and create success, would you mind sharing your story with me? My goal is to use these stories to inspire people to become achievers themselves. And I am prepared to share with you in this book what I've learned since I began investing - including all the useful tricks and tips I've picked up along the way - with anyone who cares to embark on this same journey.

Like I said earlier, if you apply what you learn here, and add to your knowledge by reading books and seeking out mentors who have done the same, the sky's the limit to what you can accomplish.

And if you do end up taking action and doing a deal, or deals, like I said, I'm really hoping you'll contact me with your story and let me know about it. I'd be very pleased to let everyone know about your success.

Note: My contact information will be at the end of the book so we can connect and you can share your success stories or contact me with questions.

Will you be one of the few that achieve success?

Certainly, you can be!

However, I am not going to tell you that it's easy. Sorry, it's really not going to be a walk in the park when you're first starting out.

You will need to commit to taking positive action - not only once - but continually until taking action becomes a habit, or even an instinct.

There will be plenty of work ahead. You will need to roll up your sleeves and get your hands dirty. However, the rewards will be truly astonishing. But once again, I warn you:

There are no 'magic pills' here!

If you're looking for a "magic pill" you can take at night so you can wake up the following morning successful, sorry, it's not here.

What you can find in this book are solid investment principles and essential tips to start you on your path to making money by flipping houses.

I hope you're OK with putting in the effort required for this venture. I'm telling you again, there's going to be work to be done. But relax, it's not going to be terribly difficult. People who have far less capabilities than you have made it in this business. I know you'll ace this if this if you follow the steps I'm going to provide.

After all, none of the work to be done is actual 'manual' labor. It's mostly going to be reading, putting together your team, analyzing and practical application.

As a matter of fact, this whole house flipping process can be quite simple if you follow the **7 Fundamentals of a Highly Successful Flip** that I am going to layout for you in this book.

I should also let you let you know that I meet people every week who are interested in flipping houses, but for some reason, only a very small percentage of them go out and do it the right way. Also, a good number of the people who claim they are interested in house flipping don't actually take the next step. They simply let it go and give up without even trying.

There are even others who go out and try to 'reinvent the wheel'. They make up their own systems and try to formulate new ways to flip a house. While I admire such bold acts, most, if not all, of these 'aspiring pioneers' end up losing big time. They actually end very, very, very badly.

My own real estate investing career was far from perfect. I made a lot of mistakes along the way - some of these mistakes were pretty drastic, not to mention, expensive. But the good news is, you don't have to relive my mistakes yourself. I already committed them, all you need to do is be smart and learn from them.

Always remember, do what has been tried and tested and proven to be successful. It's all in this book. You just have to take the time to read it, understand it and apply it.

*If you want to see some of the mistakes I've made flipping houses, go here:

www.FlipAHouseBook.com/resources

*Watch the Mistakes Video

Whatever your motivation is to learn how to flip houses, it is my purpose with this book to show you everything you need to know in order to accomplish this task with 100% success.

I will teach you all I have learned from my house flipping experiences that will include in detail how to *Find, Fund, Fix* and *Flip* houses as well as some of the other critical fundamentals.

BUT WAIT!

Before we proceed, let me give this stern **WARNING.**

I have seen a lot of people (including myself) get into real estate investing and wind up working more than when they were working a job.

DO NOT FALL INTO THIS TRAP!

One of the things that intrigued me about becoming a real estate investor was the possibility to create the 'ideal lifestyle'. I wanted to push the envelope and try to create and set up systems that can run my business for me, so I can spend most of my time with my family and pursuing greater things in life.

Not that I don't work hard in real estate. I do. All my associates can attest to it. But the difference is I don't work hard because I have to - I do it because it is something I enjoy, and more importantly, it is something that I control.

So as we progress through this book, I want you to consider establishing similar processes and systems that will allow you to set up your flips systematically and would allow for consistent cash flow, while requiring only a minimal amount of your time.

"It's not about the money you make, it's about the life you create"

-Me

After I realized that flipping a house was 'somewhat' simple if I accounted for each of the 7 Fundamentals, it was easier to systemize the process. And you know what the funny thing is? You can outsource most of the responsibilities so that flipping a house doesn't actually take up very much of your time at all.

As a matter of fact, it is recommended that you outsource most of the responsibilities of your flips after you've got your feet wet with a few deals. The converse side to this is that it is also important that you experience doing the actual work when you start out. This will allow you to better understand what part of the flipping process you need to outsource, and which part you can do yourself.

I actually completed a flip recently that took up less than 20 hours of my time. I purchased, rehabbed and sold this property in exactly 60 days, and grossed over $63,000. We also completed another one that had a net profit of over $100,000 in approximately 5 months time and I only went to the property 5 times.

Keep reading, I will show you how you can do the same.

Lastly, I want to thank you for purchasing this book.

I want to make a promise to you: As you commence reading this book, I promise that you will find usable and practical information contained within. I also promise that if you make the commitment to apply these principles with wisdom and due diligence, the possibilities of your success are unlimited!

*"At least eighty percent of millionaires are self-made.
That is, they started with nothing but ambition and energy,
the same way most of us start."*

-Brian Tracy

Are you ready?

Then Let's Get Started!

CHAPTER TWO

MINDSET

FLIP FUNDAMENTAL #1 – MINDSET

Alright, let me start by asking the #1 question on your mind right now:

Is it possible to flip a home in today's market?

YES! Despite what your family, friends and the media may tell you, it is still possible to make money flipping houses.

I know, I know. I am aware that financial markets are always volatile and unpredictable. Just recently, banks and even financial systems of entire countries were falling apart before our eyes and in the past few years we have also been witness to a mortgage meltdown like never before. Despite all this, and contrary to common knowledge, in most areas, there was NEVER a housing crisis. Rather, we simply had some financing obstacles that needed to be overcome. Nevertheless, there are still many opportunities to thrive in every market and there is still a great demand for housing in many parts of the country.

In every crisis that occurs there is always an opportunity lurking just around the corner. This quote from Joanie Warren is one of my all time favorites and really speaks to the entrepreneurial mindset that is required to thrive in real estate:

"There Are Those Who See An Opportunity, and There Are Those Who SEIZE The Opportunity"

-Joanie Warren

Case in point, during the past downturn in the economy, the media's relentless agenda to scare everyone away from real estate, created very favorable supply and demand relationships with regard to the surplus of homes in comparison to the number of home buyers.

For example, in my hometown of Houston, we experienced one of the lowest available inventory of homes in decades. Many of the 'newbie' investors got scared and left the real estate market. This allowed many of us, 'veterans', to conduct business with very little competition.

Speaking of inventory, the 'Amount of Inventory' of homes that is available in your local market is one of the key indicators that will let you know when it is a good time to flip.

For example, when the amount of inventory is low, this is good (low supply = high demand). However, when there is an increased number of homes for sale (surplus of supply = lower demand), this tends to lend itself to a "buyers" market. This means you'll have to use caution when you're flipping houses. However, don't think that just because the market is down that you can't flip houses.

Remember the Mindset quote, there is opportunity in every market. During the down markets I've been through we've always found ways to flip houses, it simply means that you should be buying them cheaper and selling them cheaper than when the market is at full-strength. We'll discuss this later in the Income Generation chapter where I'll make sure that you have multiple exit strategies and different buyer options when it comes time to list and flip your properties.

Back to the Amount of Inventory discussion, the Amount of Inventory is measured is by the number of months it takes to sell homes in that market if all new construction ceased and no other homes were listed for sale. For example, in my local market, when the inventory is less than 6 months, this is good. However, when inventory gets to be 8 to 9 months or more, flipping houses gets much more difficult. We'll dig deeper into this topic later in the book.

I know while some of you are reading this, you are eager to get started house flipping. However, you feel it is impossible to find financing for deals, or maybe you're not sure how to locate the right property to flip. Well, I can assure you there is plenty of money you can access to fund your deals, and it is possible to find real estate deals every day - even without looking for them (I'll explain how later).

Opportunities are there. They may be different depending on the market and market conditions, but they do exist. You just need to be willing to go seek them out.

The **7 Fundamentals of a Highly Successful Flip** will help you accomplish this.

DEFINITION: Fundamental- a basic principle, rule, law, or the like, that serves as the groundwork of a system; essential part: *to master the fundamentals of a trade.*

If you want to have success in any business venture, having established guidelines, or better yet, FUNDAMENTALS to help you along the decision making process is absolutely critical.

I'll be honest, when I began flipping houses, I had a lot of difficulties 'reinventing the wheel'. Sure, I had read some books and had great mentoring, but there didn't seem to be a complete system that simplified the process. There was a lot of great information I received, however, there was a lack of congruency, from start to finish, that could answer all of the questions that I had on how to flip a house.

So I diligently began to put together systems and a formula that would create repeated positive results. My goal was to build a systematized business and create repetitive cash flow over and over again.

Now, let me share with you the 7 fundamental areas of flipping that I have discovered that will most greatly affect your success and profitability:

7 Fundamentals of a Highly Successful Flip

Finding — ✓ Mindset
✓ Deal Flow
✓ Evaluating Deals
✓ Estimating Repairs
Funding — ✓ Financing
Fixing — ✓ Rehabbing
Flipping — ✓ Income Generation

You noticed above that I have 4 side notations:

1. Finding (Deal Flow)

2. Financing

3. Rehabbing

4. Flipping

If you've read other books or articles on real estate flipping, you've probably seen a similar categorization of these 4 steps. In a nutshell, these four steps must be successfully carried out to achieve a profit. PERIOD.

However, in my opinion, if you don't have other key ingredients intertwined with these 4 steps, you're not going to succeed. The difference in why some people achieve success and others fail, has to do with the information that is within the 'gaps' of these 'common' knowledge steps.

It's kind of like a good hamburger. If you only have some meat and a bun, it's not going to be that great. But if you have the right seasoning, with lettuce, cheese, tomato and maybe a few jalapenos on top, then you're going to start salivating!

So, that's what we're looking to achieve with the flip process, we're gonna season it up and throw on some of the fixins' that will make it absolutely irresistible!

You see, if I only told you how to execute the *basics* of house flipping, to be honest, that would be a huge disservice. This is because it's going to be the intangibles that will set you apart from the rest of your competition. These additional fundamentals are what will help you overcome the challenges you're going to meet along the way.

So in addition to going over the basics of Finding - Financing - Rehabbing - Flipping, we'll also fill in the blanks along the way like making offers, filling out contracts, conducting inspections and a whole slew of other incidental yet necessary activities.

So, when flipping a house, just keep in mind all of the 7 fundamentals. Doing so will allow you the greatest chance of succeeding in this business. Make sense? Good, then let's get started!

FLIP FUNDAMENTAL #1 - MINDSET

Before we get too entrenched in the real estate side of things, I would like to share with you what is, by far, the most important success factor when flipping a house. I urge you to give me just a few moments of your undivided attention as we discuss what I consider to be the 'secret' ingredient as to why some people achieve success, and others fall short.

When flipping houses (as with all things in life), there are going to be obstacles along the way. All great achievers in the past have had to overcome obstacles at some point in time in order to achieve success.

Real Estate is no exception to this rule.

While there really are easy flips that offer very minimal challenges, you need to understand right from the get go that this will not always be the case. In fact, most flips will not be a walk in the park.

If you plan on being in the house flipping business, or any business for that matter, for any length of time, you will experience occasional setbacks along the way.

One of my coaches often says, "Life and Business become incredibly simple and easy when you acknowledge that Life & Business will never be easy". So yea, it's kind of like that :)

What separates those who will thrive and those who will collapse under pressure, is not only the individuals personal experience and knowledge, but also (and perhaps, more importantly) their personal mindset and determination.

If your mindset is marked by a determination to accomplish a goal NO MATTER WHAT, then you will most likely achieve success.

Problem is, most people fear failure to the point that they refuse to even lift a finger and try.

I want you take a few moments to think about what your current mindset is when it comes to successfully flipping houses.

What if you run into troubles along the way? (I can guarantee you, troubles will come) Will you give up? Or, will you push through and find the solution to the challenge at hand?

I can tell you from experience, there is no challenge that is insurmountable. Commit yourself to developing and strengthening your mindset. Make a commitment to yourself that you will not give up, quit or run away when you meet challenges. Instead, you will face any obstacle that presents itself and commit to achieving success.

"Whether you think you can, or think you can't, you're right"

-Henry Ford

Believe me, I know how it feels the first time you decide to flip a house - it's SCARY. Not even the promise of wealth is enough to obscure the fear of failure and the possibility of financial loss. It is this same fear that stops a lot of people from taking affirmative action.

But I'm telling you now: **Don't let fear rule your life.**

I don't know about you, but I am more haunted by the fear of never trying, rather than the fear of failing when I take a chance at something. I look at it this way: If I try and do something, there's a

50% chance I'll fail, but there's also a 50% chance I'll succeed. However, if I don't try at all, even that 50% chance of succeeding disappears and I'm just guaranteeing that failure wins hands down.

Anytime you hear FEAR start talking to you with that familiar voice inside your head, use this acronym:

FEAR is only False Evidence Appearing Real

You've probably heard that before, but the simple fact is we are all going to experience fear at some point in time. It is a certainty that there will be occasions when we will be afraid.

You may be afraid of doing something different. You may be afraid of losing money. You may be afraid of quitting your job. You may most likely be afraid of flipping your first house. When you begin to feel fear, it's important that you recognize it and seek to find out if those fears are well founded and likely to occur, which may be the case sometimes, or just obnoxious stories that you've created for yourself.

There are essentially 2 types of Fear:

1. Useful

2. Non-Useful

Useful fear is like the feeling you get if you're about to touch a hot stove. Of course, your body is going to react very usefully to try to get you to not touch the hot burner because of the pain and injury that can result. However in real estate, most times, we're dealing with a lot of 'Non-Useful' fear stories that we create that have no validity whatsoever.

Like I said, most times, the fear we experience is totally false and unfounded and should be discarded immediately. Les Brown, one of the most renowned motivational speakers says that too many of us are not living our dreams because we are living our fears. So I personally make it a point to acknowledge when I am experiencing fear and dissect it to find out if it is a serious threat, or just something I can hit the 'delete' button on and move forward and take action.

Another source of Fear generation when something new arises that we don't understand or aren't familiar with. This is a much more primitive reaction, and thus, a bit more difficult to curb. Understand that this is a normal reaction for people trying to get out of their comfort zones. When you've already grown so accustomed to a particular pattern and routine in your life, even if the routine causes discomfort, and something new comes along that forces us out of our familiar patterns, we normally react negatively with fear.

But the good news is, most new things and experiences we encounter that may appear overly complex usually just takes a little education to understand. And with the abundance of learning techniques and resources available to us now, the aforementioned complexity has already been greatly reduced. With the right education and mentorship, most, if not all, projects can be broken down into small bite size pieces, thus rendering them more simple and making the goals they represent as a whole much more achievable.

One purpose of this book is to serve as your 'House Flipping Fear Conqueror' and help you break down the steps of house flipping in order to make the process more simple and systematized.

To this effect, I can boldly affirm that fear is nothing more than a lack of knowledge and experience. This is because when you begin to equip yourself with the right knowledge and information, the initial fear begins to subside until it gets supplanted by confidence and encouragement.

Did you know that Michael Jordan was cut from his high school basketball team? What if he quit playing basketball then? What if he let the fear of failure get the upper hand and he just bowed down to it?

Well, he didn't quit. And as a result, he went on to have what in my opinion, and most others, was the greatest career in professional basketball.

I love this quote from Michael Jordan:

"I've missed more than 9,000 shots in my career. I've lost almost 300 games. 26 times, I've been trusted to take the game winning shot and missed. I've failed over and over and over again in my life. And that is why I succeed."

-Michael Jordan

That is a great example of a mindset that is focused on success. He wasn't afraid to take the game winning shot, even though he knew there was a possibility of failure.

This type of mindset can be applied to many different areas, if not the entirety, of our lives. And that includes, of course, flipping a house.

For years even before I began investing in real estate, I would often daydream about breaking away from my job to become a full time entrepreneur and to pursue a life of excitement and riches. But most of the time, I stopped at the daydream and failed to follow through with decisive and affirmative action to make it come true.

It was not until I became TOTALLY FOCUSED on my goal, that I began to achieve success. Amazingly, the moment I made up my mind and fully committed to achieving greatness, things began to fall into place. At the same exact time, my fear began to subside and I began to take action steps to achieving my goals with confidence and encouragement.

"A good plan, violently executed now, is better than a perfect plan next week"

-George S. Patton

Don't worry about not having the perfect plan of action. This is another common roadblock that keeps people from moving forward in their entrepreneurial projects. While it is true that it is essential to have a good plan of attack when planning your business ventures, you should not fall into the trap of over thinking and over planning. If you do, chances are, you'll get so overwhelmed by the details, you'll be too afraid to even take a single step.

Remember this: there is no perfect plan because you can never prepare for all contingencies. As long as you have a well, thought of plan that has been put together logically, commit to putting it in action and then just do it. You'll have plenty of time to straighten out the rough spots as you go and it will become a great learning experience for you. Don't worry about committing mistakes along the way, especially if you're starting out. You'll get better at it eventually. Just don't be frozen by fear into a state of inaction.

"I am an old man and have known many great troubles, and most of them, never happened"

-Mark Twain

Don't let fear and the "what-ifs" keep you from reaching your desired and deserved success. Counteract these fears with a solid knowledge base and never underestimate the power of a strong and determined mindset.

By combining the proper knowledge and skills (which you will soon have after reading this book), with your determined mindset, you will have created a formula for success you'll be able to use over and over again.

Now Let's Talk About Flipping Some Houses!

CHAPTER THREE

DEAL FLOW

FLIP FUNDAMENTAL #2 – DEAL FLOW

If you are on limited time (I know, who isn't?) like I was when I started flipping houses, it is imperative you do not waste time looking for deals.

I have seen a lot of new investors spend way too much time looking through classified ads, local real estate magazines and even worse, driving all over town spending hours and hours searching for deals.

This is NOT what successful flippers do!

These activities are more in line with what I like to call a J-O-B! If you want to have true success in this business, **you must make the deals come to you through the actions of others.**

I will repeat that: If you want to have true success in this business, you must make the deals come to you through the actions of others.

Here's a quote from John Maxwell that frames it well:

"A good leader (or entrepreneur) never puts off until tomorrow something they can have someone else do today"

You must quickly learn to utilize OPT (Other Peoples Time) to bring you deals. This is what is called "Deal Flow." The idea behind this is simple: the more deals that are flowing to you, the more opportunities you will have to flip houses.

This doesn't mean that you buy every deal that comes your way. That's a big NO. What this means is that once you have an abundance of deals flowing your way, you can 'cherry pick' the best ones to ensure a hefty payday. It's not uncommon for me to say no to dozens of deals that come across my desk before I find something really worth pursuing that I end up signing a contract for to purchase. I would recommend you do the same.

It is true that there are dozens of ways you can find deals on your own. The problem, however, is you need to have the time and desire to drive all over town to check out the deals, or go to auctions and bid on houses yourself, or put together marketing blitzes/mailers you have to send out yourself, or spend hours taking countless phone calls from sellers - all these, just to find a deal.

Yes, there can be money made and nice deals to be found by "doing it yourself" and finding deals using some of the activities mentioned above. But this is NOT an ideal approach for newbie flippers and it is NOT the focus of this book. Nor is this how I got started in this business.

I want this book to be a guide for you to create a business system that works - that is, a system that does most of the grunt work for you while you work less, and still rake in the big checks.

I'd hate to see you suffer the same fate as a number of newbie investors I have come across where they put together marketing campaigns all by themselves, or some who went to auctions without really having a strong understanding of how that works, and such other activities - only to end up several months later with still no deal to show for their hard work.

I want to clarify something real quick before we move forward about direct marketing. I'm a big believer in marketing and creating paid marketing campaigns to find deals and we will touch on this in this book. However, I want to be clear, it is very important in the beginning for those of you already pressed for time with work, family life, etc., that you make a clear decision to embrace this lesson of utilizing others to bring you deals. Creating marketing campaigns and responding to leads takes a tremendous amount of time and effort and is almost like an entirely different business model. So my focus in this book is aimed at creating deal flow from the activities of others.

So lets talk about the ideal scenario here, which is to create a business that will generate deals to come to you and not the other way around - that's what I want to share with you.

Here are some of the ways you can do this:

WEBSITES

There are literally hundreds of websites that list properties for sale. Without a doubt, when utilized properly, the Internet is an incredibly powerful tool and should be considered a good source to find deals.

I have found websites that are locally run and maintained are typically better than some of the nationwide mass marketed websites.

Just do a quick Google search for 'real estate deals' with your city name as well and you'll most likely find several sites with some potential deals in your area.

However, if a really good deal is posted on the Internet, you can bet there is going to be a lot of competition. And keep in mind, if a deal gets listed on a popular website and it isn't sold fast, then more than likely, this is not a good deal because good deals move fast. The occasional exception to this rule is if the listing doesn't sell fast, and becomes 'stale' and the price gets dropped, in which case it may be a good idea to swoop in and snag the deal.

Some websites have a 'property tracker' option where you can get email notifications whenever there are updates or new listings.

Another thing to remember when sourcing deals through websites, is that just because a property is listed for a certain price, doesn't mean that you have to offer that price. Take all listed prices at merely a starting point for negotiations. We'll discuss making offers and negotiations at the end of this chapter.

While websites are a fairly good source for deals, this is not my preferred choice. What I recommend is for you to keep an eye on a few websites that suit your needs and devote a small part of your time browsing through them. There are far better options to find deals and it is best to reserve your focus on these methods.

REAL ESTATE AGENTS

One of the first steps you can take in creating deal flow is building a team of 'investor experienced' real estate agents that know exactly the type of deals you are looking for.

I have been fortunate to have some really good agents as part of my team over the years. I've also had to 'weed out' some of the others that didn't quite understand what I was looking for, but the point is, you need real estate agents on your team who know the game you're playing and are willing to play it with you.

When building your team of agents, you must make sure they understand the types of deals you are looking for and they must be willing to occasionally submit low offers.

Just so you know, some Realtors do not like to submit low offers, and consequently, may not be the best fit in helping you find the best deal. So make sure when you work with real estate agents, they understand that you are only looking for deals with significant discounts and you would rarely consider paying list price for anything - unless, of course, the numbers make total sense.

Ideally, I prefer working with agents that have personal experience investing in real estate. I have found that agents who've purchased investment properties for themselves are less likely to waste your time because they know what your business is about right off the bat. Moreover, when they call you about a house, it tends to be a more viable deal than what a non-investor agent may bring forth. As a matter of fact, several of the agents that I work with are very active investors, so they really know how to analyze a deal. This means, if they are calling me about it, there is a good chance I may have found my next flip project.

Some people might ask, why would a real estate agent would "pass off" a property if it is in fact a great deal, instead of just flipping it themselves? Great question and I assure you, there are many possible reasons for this. First, some agents may prefer or need the quick cash/commission as opposed to the longer term, higher risk, profit of flipping. Moreover, some flips are too large or may involve more capital than some agents may have access to. Furthermore, some agents may view a deal to be "too risky" and they may want to hand it off to a more experienced investor, for a fee of course.

There are many reasons people pass deals along to other investors. But the important point is, who cares what their motivation is. A deal is a deal.

Another advantage of having real estate agents in your network is being able to find out who the top performers are in the neighborhoods you are considering to set up shop in. You can do this by searching the web or calling out yard signs. The top agents in any given neighborhood most likely run across deals in that neighborhood. You just need to make sure they put you on their 'short list' of investors they can call whenever they have viable deals available. This can work out great for you when realtors run across properties that need more repairs that the average homebuyer or a novice investor would be interested in taking on.

WHERE TO FIND REAL ESTATE AGENTS

The easiest way to find agents is by going online to see what brokerages and agents have listings in your targeted areas.

Go on a local website that has houses for sale in your area. Start calling agents and brokers whose contact information appears on the website (Hint: The more instances you see an agent or a broker's name, chances are, that person is active). Start interviewing agents you feel you'll be able to work with.

You can also meet real estate agents at your local real estate investment clubs and real estate networking events. This is how I have met most of the agents I work with.

CONTACTING REAL ESTATE AGENTS

When initiating contact with real estate agents, keep in mind that you should be sincere and honest. Tell them about yourself and your investing experience. You don't have to hide anything from them. If you've never done a deal before, be upfront and let them know you are a beginner. However, don't sell yourself short. Let them know that you are highly motivated, equipped and ready to proceed as soon as the right deal comes your way.

Make sure to touch on your personal and professional details as well (i.e., educational background, professional background etc.) just to establish some credibility. Remember not to appear to be bragging or all knowing.

It's also important to let them know your financing plans for the flip. Nothing turns off an agent from working with you more than the uncertainty of how you're going to finance a deal when one actually comes your way. We'll talk more about financing later in this book.

Here is an example of how this first conversation may sound:

"Hello, my name is _____ and I am looking to develop a relationship with an agent that can help me find some good investment properties to flip. I am looking for deals that are deeply discounted from their true value, usually because they are in need of serious repairs. I prefer them to be in good neighborhoods with good schools. Would you mind putting me on your email or call list for whenever you run across a home that meets this criteria?"

When you have an agent conversation that goes well, and you think you may have found a good 'fit' with the agent you just spoke with, be sure to do a follow-up phone call or email with them at the soonest possible time to let them know that you are a legitimate buyer and you're very serious about them sending deals your way.

On the other hand, when you come across an agent who's rude, has a smug attitude or someone who acts like you're wasting his time, don't sweat it. Just cross them off your list and move on to the next one. Believe me, there are more than enough agents out there. You should be looking for agents that you get along with and who are going to bring you closer to a big payday.

Also, as you begin to build your team of agents, always be respectful of their time and efforts. Understand that if you do nothing but ask them to submit offers and you never buy a house from them, they will soon lose their zeal to keep writing offers for you.

One good strategy to use when dealing with agents is to let them know that if they bring you a deal you end up buying, you'll have them list the property up for resale as soon as it gets fixed up. Make sure you are clear about this because it will definitely boost their motivation to work with you as this is an opportunity for them to earn 'double commissions'. We'll discuss strategies on listing and marketing your property in later on in the *Flip* section of this book.

Lastly, keep in mind that agents have access to a lot of valuable information you will need in order to make informed decisions about the deals you are considering. A huge part of your success depends upon the relationships that you establish with your team of agents.

Even if you are able to find only one good agent, this can still result in you making lots of money and dramatically increasing your deal flow. So, if you find a good one, do your best to cultivate that relationship and show respect and appreciation for their efforts. Of course, the greatest reward you can give them is to buy some houses from them when they bring you good ones.

Here are some of the characteristics of good investor-friendly real estate agents:

- Willingness to show you multiple properties

- Willingness to take time to answer any questions you may have

- Willingness to write offers as you see fit

- Provides full disclosure of all pertinent information

- They bring the good deals to you first!

Now, let's take a look at a way I stumbled upon on how to find deals. This method has proven to be very effective in finding deals and dramatically increasing my deal flow and by far the #1 way that I have created deal flow.

WHOLESALERS

Almost every town in America will have wholesalers that specialize in helping local investors find good deals.

A wholesaler is an individual who utilizes different marketing strategies to locate deeply discounted properties. As soon a wholesaler finds a good deal, he will put the property under contract and sell the contract to an investor for a fee.

Wholesalers are a lot like real estate agents, but they don't necessarily have a real estate license. Moreover, wholesalers specialize in working exclusively with investors.

Some wholesalers do have a real estate agent's license, but others do not because they don't actually sell houses. Instead, they sell their position in a contract that gives the investor the option to purchase a home.

Wholesalers avoid competition by going straight to the source (the homeowner selling the house) and cutting out a lot of the markup that occurs when middlemen (realtors and/or brokers) get involved and before the property gets to the MLS (Multiple Listing Service). Let me explain.

Have you ever seen signs on street corners and billboards that look similar to this:

A lot of times, these signs and billboards are the marketing efforts of a local wholesaler who is looking for people with distressed properties or, for whatever reason, are in a difficult situation and they are willing to sell their property at a substantial discount.

When a wholesaler finds a good deal, they will sign a contract with the seller and put an option in the contract that they can sell their position within the contract to someone else. The profit they sell their position for is called an **assignment fee**.

After a wholesaler has the signed contract, they begin contacting their pool of investors to see who is interested in buying the house.

Typically, assignment fees range from around $5,000 to $10,000. There are cases where you'll have to pay substantially more especially is the deal is really very good. But on the other hand, there are also cases where I've paid $500-$1,000 for the assignment fee.

I have heard some investors complain about paying excessive assignment fees to wholesalers. I don't understand this. If the deal the wholesaler has under contract, meets their buying criteria (we'll discuss the correct buying formula guidelines in the next chapter), then it shouldn't matter what the assignment fee is. As long as you the flipper, can make your profit. Besides, when analyzing a deal brought by a wholesaler, the assignment fee should already be included in the purchase price you are using to analyze the deal, so it represents no additional cost to you.

To focus on the wholesaler's assignment fee and not your own profit as an investor is faulty logic in my opinion. If you are going to make your target profit margin on a deal, does it matter what the wholesaler is making? It doesn't make sense to pass up a profit and pay more on the MLS just because you don't like the idea of wholesalers making money.

Also, keep in mind all of the work and effort that goes into the work wholesalers perform to put a home under contract. Wholesalers pay substantial marketing expenses for every deal they acquire (typically around $3,000 per contract), not to mention countless hours of negotiating with sellers, the majority of which won't even end up as deals. Look at it this way, negotiating with sellers is an absolute pain, and to be honest, most people don't have the stomach for dealing with all the emotional issues and instability of people who are facing foreclosure and other difficult life situations. So a person who is willing to do all of that stuff, all day, every day, deserves a decent wage.

As I mentioned above, most wholesalers typically find their deals directly from homeowners who are willing to substantially discount the price of their home for a myriad of reasons. They find these homes from different types of sellers. The house could be from an estate sale, someone who is behind on their mortgage or a landlord who just wants to get rid of the house. There are a lot of different reasons people sell their houses at a significant discount.

A lot of new investors have a hard time believing people will sell their home for huge discounts in comparison to what the property is really worth. My saying on this is, just because they think it's hard to believe doesn't mean it isn't true. It is absolutely true and I see it and experience it firsthand all the time.

Some of the larger wholesaling organizations will get their deals directly from banks that are discounting the price of the home, or sometimes they will get 'bulk' listings of properties. This usually happens when a bank is trying to dump a lot of properties, and is willing to discount the price to a brokerage or organization they know can sell them fast.

"The deal of the century happens everyday"

-Author, Unknown

Another great advantage of working with wholesalers is when they bring a deal to you; they generally won't waste your time.

This is generally the case, due to the fact that the wholesaler should already have the house under contract, so you don't have to submit an offer and play the 'waiting game' or get into negotiations. And if you're working with an experienced, reputable wholesaler, they will usually have an estimated repair list/cost and a comparable sales list with other properties that have sold in the area.

The wholesalers and agents who work with me know that if the deal is good, I will buy it, close quickly and not waste their time, so it's worth it to them to discount it a little more for me in order to sell it fast. And more importantly, if they bring me 'duds', they're going to tarnish their own reputation. Besides, I wouldn't buy a bad deal and they know that already.

As you build your own reputation as a serious investor who closes quickly, you will also begin to see increased deal flow from wholesalers and save time in the process.

FLIPPERS BEWARE

I'm not trying to scare you here, but there are some bad people in the world.

So, when a deal is brought to you by a wholesaler or real estate agent for that matter, ALWAYS perform your own due diligence to verify the information.

Unfortunately, I have seen investors get taken advantage of and buy deals that have not been "as advertised". This is something that can be easily avoided by verifying the information that has been provided to you.

As with any investment deal, the burden of due diligence is on the investor to verify the value of the property and the estimate of repairs for the rehab. This means you should ALWAYS do your own homework before you make a decision. And, if the numbers check out, then it may be a deal.

Like I said, the purpose is not to scare anyone. Most of the wholesalers and agents I work with bring the deals to me at really deep discounts, which I really like. However, there are always going to be exceptions to every rule, so just be careful out there.

WHERE TO FIND WHOLESALERS

I have found the best way of locating wholesalers is by networking at your local real estate investment clubs and real estate networking events.

If you're not sure where to find a local real estate networking event, check out the National Real Estate Investing Association's website www.NationalREIA.com to find a list of endorsed investment clubs across the country. This is how I have met most of my team of wholesalers.

Now that I have built these relationships with local wholesalers, I have deals being sent to me multiple times a day.

Does this mean I buy houses from dozens and dozens of wholesalers? No, not really. In practice, I typically buy about 80% of my deals from less than five wholesalers. I could definitely buy from more, because I receive a lot of emails and phone calls from other wholesalers every week, if not every day, offering me deals.

Although I will occasionally buy from other wholesalers outside of my normal team, especially if the deal is really good, I make it a point to always check out deals from my "inside team" first. This is because I already have an established relationship and process with my team and they will usually call me first with the really nice deals so this is more than enough to keep me busy buying houses. Plus, it says a lot about loyalty.

Another way to meet local wholesalers, without having to go to meetings, is by calling up those "We Buy Houses" ads and signs.

I recommend you call those signs and inform the person who answers that you are an active investor looking for deals and ask them to contact you when they have a deal that fits your criteria. This is an excellent way of initiating first contact with local wholesalers and can definitely develop into a good working relationship.

You can also visit certain websites to look for deals and wholesalers. One of the best that I have seen is www.MyHouseDeals.com. Essentially, this website is a forum for wholesalers to post their deals for investors. So this is a good resource to find and meet local wholesalers.

Don't fall into the trap of thinking you need to have dozens of real estate agents and wholesalers to bring you deals. When starting out, it's okay to just find 1 good wholesaler or real estate agent. After all, you'd want to concentrate on quality over quantity. One wholesaler or real estate agent that consistently brings you good deals is better than an entire army of them bringing you nothing but lemons.

OTHER POSSIBLE DEAL SOURCES

Although the core lead generation will most likely come from wholesalers and Realtors, every so often, you're going to have a good deals fall in your lap, especially once you begin networking and meeting other investors and real estate professionals. As you begin to establish your reputation, you never know who'll give you a lead for a deal. This can come from other investors, appraisers, lenders, inspectors, contractors, or just friends and acquaintances.

I recently bought a home from a lady that works out at the same CrossFit gym as me. She had heard that I was a house flipper and her mother needed to sell her home and long story short, were able to workout a deal that both sides were happy with. Like I said, things like this won't be your main source of deal flow, but as you get more established, deal flow will begin to come to you from a number of sources.

THE RULE OF ONE

If you are just starting out, I want to eliminate a lot of the workload you may be subconsciously imposing on yourself by thinking you need to do more than you really do.

In the beginning, I want you to focus on just finding one really good agent or wholesaler. This may be the only person you need to get started with your first flip.

As a matter of fact, I bought my very first property from a wholesaler I met at a local real estate investment club and I bought nine more houses from him that same year. I have gone on to buy over 40 properties from his company since that time. This is a good example of how one good contact can be infinitely more valuable than dozens or possibly hundreds of other "okay" contacts.

I can honestly say, because I have a great team of wholesalers an Realtors, that I spend very little (if any) of my time actively looking for deals. I want your business to operate like this as well.

The funny thing is, if you really focus on finding just one good agent or wholesaler to bring you deals and it's an individual that you work well with, the word will soon spread that you are a 'real' buyer.

As you begin to do more deals and networking, other wholesalers and agents will find out who you are and start seeking you out in order to bring deals to you. You will begin to have agents and wholesalers call and email you deals on a frequent basis and will have more deal flow than you could possibly handle. This is what I like to call, a *Good Problem* to have!

And it all starts with just finding 1 good deal finder.

SUMMARY

Lastly, I want to reiterate something I mentioned at the start of this chapter. I have seen a lot of new investors get started by trying to find their own deals and doing direct marketing in the beginning of their business, but they get tired and burnt out before finding their first deal. I think that if you have a desire to do direct marketing, you may want to consider starting off as a Wholesaler and specialize in that aspect of the business until you reach mastery or get to a level that you're ready to branch into the investing/flipping side of things.

Can you do both? Absolutely, but only if you have the time and resources that each aspect of the business requires. Although, if you're working a full-time job and have a family and other responsibilities, it is incredibly difficult to do both direct marketing and running an investment/flipping business. This is why I strongly urge you to consider developing relationships with Agents and Wholesalers so you can begin to have deals flowing to you with just a little time investment on your part. This will allow you to move closer to being a true real estate investor, instead of spending your days behind a windshield driving neighborhoods and looking for houses to flip.

Regardless of how you find your deals, whatever you do, EXERCISE PATIENCE! Don't try to force a deal because you are anxious, do your due diligence, analyze the numbers, THEN, if the numbers make sense, you can move forward and sign the contract.

Here is a review of the Key Points to Finding A Deal:

WEBSITES - Websites that are locally run and maintained are typically better than most of the nationwide websites

REAL ESTATE AGENTS - Make sure they know the types of properties you are looking for and be respectful of their efforts as you cultivate your team of agents.

WHOLESALERS - Use reputable wholesalers that provide accurate information and deals that fit your criteria.

JUST FIND 1 - Start by finding just one good wholesaler or real estate agent to bring you just one deal.

CHAPTER FOUR

EVAULATING DEALS

FLIP FUNDAMENTAL #3 – EVAULATING DEALS

If you're going to make money on a flip - which I hope is your goal - then you must make a promise to yourself to do exactly that.

And to this end I ask you to raise your right hand and repeat after me:

"I, (State Your Name) do solemnly swear to NEVER buy a property unless it meets and/or exceeds the buying formula that Brant is about to lay on me. Even during times when I get really, really emotionally involved with a house and the numbers don't even make sense BUT because I'm anxious to do a deal and it kind of 'looks' like an 'ok' deal even though when I plug in the numbers to Brant's formula it doesn't work out YET I am STILL considering buying the house, HOWEVER, because I've made this promise to Brant right here and now, I, Insert Name, do solemnly swear not to buy the house unless it meets and/or exceeds Brant's buying formula. Never. The End."

Ok, all joking aside, the point here is that you need to exercise self-control and don't prematurely buy a deal unless the numbers make good business sense. If you pull the trigger too soon and get locked into a 'bad deal' you could find yourself aboard a loser and it can sink you real quick.

Ever seen Titanic? :-)

Enough of that, let's go over the formula I want you to use to properly analyze a deal to verify if a house is worthy to be a *Flipper*.

I want to make this clear: Learning this simple formula is fundamental to your knowledge base, and applying this principle will have a tremendous impact on your success. In a moment, we'll go more in depth with some of the real estate terms you'll need to familiarize yourself with.

Here is the formula:

70% of After Repairs Value (ARV) - Repair Costs = Maximum Offer (MO)

So, in other words, if someone brings you a deal that is worth $100,000 after it is all fixed up (ARV), and it needs $20,000 in repairs:

$70,000 (70% ARV) - $20,000 (Repair Costs) = $50,000 Maximum Offer (MO)

As you will soon learn, most of the deals you analyze will require at least basic repairs to get them back on the market for resale. You'll even come across a lot of deals that will require major repairs.

In this example, we estimated the repairs to be $20,000. We then subtracted $20,000 from $70,000, which is 70% of our After Repair Value to arrive at our final Maximum Offer of $50,000. Of course, if you can get deals for less than the 70% ARV, then the more profit you can make.

Can I Do Deals Above The 70% Line?

The 70% ARV Standard was the accepted and used ratio for many years, and it provides a nice profit margin with room for error, but just as Bob Dylan would say, "The times they are a changin."

To answer a question I'm sure more than a few of you have, YES, there are times we buy properties to Flip above the 70% line and this number is not set in stone. But as a real estate investor and coach to others, this is simply the Formula that we use to know for sure if a house is a deal or not for our Company, but understand that markets vary greatly and fluctuate constantly, so this number may float higher or lower, but not significantly. As I write this book, we are currently going up to 75% on some deals, but I think this is about as high as you should ever consider going because the profit margins begin to get to thin and risky at this point.

There are many additional factors that will come into play when deciding on taking on a deal above the 70% ARV range such as:

- Are you financing the property or using cash?

- If financing, what are the terms?

- How hot is that particular market?

- What price point is the home selling?

- Do you have other exit strategies if this deal doesn't flip quickly?

However, for the "new" investors, the formula of **70% of ARV - Repairs**, is a good 'safety' zone to stay under as you start your investing career. As you gain more knowledge and experience, you can calculate your own risk versus reward. Make sense? Good.

By the way, don't worry about how to estimate the cost of repairs just yet. We will cover that in the next chapter.

I want to reiterate that using this formula is absolutely critical when you're first getting started. If the maximum offer price exceeds 70% of the ARV, you are putting yourself at risk of not making a profit. I don't think I need to tell you that you wouldn't want to put yourself in that position, besides, you made a vow to me just a few minutes ago, remember?

My hope is that you will not become emotionally persuaded when looking at properties and making decisions on purchasing a flip property. So, if you choose to go above that 70% range, just make sure you've really done your homework before moving forward.

Buying a house and using the buying formula should be a strict business formality. You have to become proficient at letting the formula help you make a good business decision on whether you buy a house or not. Let me help you out with a link to make this analysis process a bit easier:

www.FlipAHouseBook.com/Resources

*See the "FreeFlipAnalyzer" on the resources page

Example Deal from FreeFlipAnalyer

Input YELLOW Highlighted AREAS ONLY		
Project Name: 123 Flip St.		
Property Value (ARV)		100,000
Purchase Price		50,000
Repairs		20,000
Loan (monthly)		700
Insurance (monthly)		50
Taxes (monthly)		250
Misc. (utilities, maintenance)		150
Closing Costs (buy)		$1,400
*Add Origination Points (if necessary) here		1,400
Closing Costs (sell)		$1,250
Realtors Commission		$6,000

*Realtors Commission is using a Standard 6% Listing/Commission paid to the Realtors.
If you are using a flat fee listing, you can reduce your closing costs by 3% off the total sales price

Total Costs WITHOUT Any Holding Costs:	$81,200
GROSS PROFIT	**$18,800**

HOLDING TIME	Holding Costs	Gross Profit	
2 months	$2,300	Gross Profit	$16,500
3 months	$3,450	Gross Profit	$15,350
4 months	$4,600	Gross Profit	$14,200
5 months	$5,750	Gross Profit	$13,050
6 months	$6,900	Gross Profit	$11,900
7 months	$8,050	Gross Profit	$10,750
8 months	$9,200	Gross Profit	$9,600
9 months	$10,350	Gross Profit	$8,450
10 months	$11,500	Gross Profit	$7,300
11 months	$12,650	Gross Profit	$6,150
12 months	$13,800	Gross Profit	$5,000

It's as simple as this:

1. Input the numbers into the formula.

2. If the numbers work, proceed with the deal.

3. If the numbers don't work, walk away.

You have to become proficient about letting the numbers tell the story and guide your decision, and follow suit by walking away from deals when the numbers don't work.

This is one of those 'thin lines' between success and failure. If you stray too far from this formula and do some bad deals you may not make it back, so use caution my friends.

"You've got to know when to hold 'em, Know when to fold 'em,

Know when to walk away, Know when to run"

-Kenny Rogers, "The Gambler"

TRASH IN, TRASH OUT

There is a saying that goes along the lines of, "whatever goes in, comes out" or "trash in, trash out". This should always be in your mind when working your numbers on your deals.

The formula will not and cannot work unless the numbers you are putting in are valid numbers. If the numbers you are using are not accurate, then of course the 'story' your numbers are telling will be false. It is essential you use only verified data when putting in numbers into the formula.

So, how do you get "good numbers"? Before we answer that question, let's make sure we're up to speed with the key terms we're using here:

ARV or "After Repair Value" is the price the house will be worth after it has been fixed. Remember, I told you a while ago that most of the houses you end up buying will need some sort of repairs before they're ready to be put back in the market either as a rental or as a flip property. The cost of these repairs needs to be factored in to your evaluation. The key to finding an accurate ARV is to base valuations from comps.

Comps stands for Comparables. This can represent Comparable Sales & Leases, or Comparable Market Value. Basically, this is how much similar properties have actually sold in the same general area as the property you are considering buying. You will find these from local real estate agents or Internet based software.

You do not want to make the mistake of basing the value of a home from the county tax records, or, what current properties may be listed for. You MUST base the value from similar properties within the given area that have actually SOLD recently, preferably within in the last 1 – 6 months.

Some neighborhoods may not have houses that have sold in the last 6 months because they're not very large neighborhoods or there hasn't been much activity. Also, there may be VERY low turnover because they are in high demand. In these cases, you may be required to look further into the past, possibly even going back a year or so to find comparable sales data. Just be sure to keep in mind financial climates change and affect sales at different periods of time, so it's always best to use recent comps. If you have a relationship with a realtor that will pull comps for you, then this can be done in a matter of minutes.

MO or "Maximum Offer" is just that - it is the maximum offer recommended to make on the property after you determine your cost of repairs and the ARV. You may also see this as the acronym, MAO, which stands for Maximum Allowable Offer.

Like I said, your MO should generally not exceed 70% ARV minus cost of repairs, but it doesn't mean that you have to settle for 70%.

To be honest, when the market is down, you should be getting deals in the 60-65% ARV minus cost of repairs range. This is for a couple of reasons: First, the Days On Market (DOM) it takes to sell a property during a down market is longer. Secondly, because you can!

Remember that a deeper discount at which you buy translates into more profit when you sell. So if you can get an ARV that's lower than 70%, go on right ahead and take it.

An exception to this rule is when you locate a property in a really hot market with a low DOM. This means deals in the area sell a lot quicker than your normal deals. You may be OK with going slightly above the 70% ARV because the faster turnaround will basically compensate for the slightly lower profit. Look at it this way, if you can get the deal and make $3,000 - $5,000 less than you think you should, but close the deal in half the time than your normal turnaround (15 days instead of 30 days or 30 days instead of 60 days), it wouldn't be too bad of a deal, right?

But once again, I repeat, please use caution. And as soon as you determine your MO, stick with it. Don't let your emotions take over and give in. If the seller doesn't want to budge on the price, so be it, don't go above the buying formula. Stick to your guns and walk away. There are plenty of deals out there.

AFTER REPAIR VALUE

To determine the ARV, you first have to get a list of comps that have sold recently in that area.

Remember when I said it's good to have some real estate agent contacts? This is precisely the reason why. Licensed real estate agents have access to comps in their particular market areas that they're licensed to practice in. If you have an agent you can call, getting accurate comps is super easy, and it can be had in a matter of minutes. If not, you'll have to find a website that can provide you comps to help you out. One that I like is www.ZipRealty.com. There are many of them, so don't fret. Also, I want to warn you that if you're using websites to base your valuation on, be sure to verify your findings with accurate Comps from the MLS. There is really no substitute to the MLS.

You must also make sure you have accurate comps. Meaning, the comps you are using must be as similar to your target property as possible. The comps do not have to be exact, but they should be similar or as close as possible to being the same.

Now, this is not an exact science and there are some definite grey areas here, so bare with me. So what does a similar Comp look like? Let's look at some of the key areas that make a comp, a comp:

Here are some of the critical areas to compare:

- Square Footage

- Year of Construction

- Features (number of bedrooms/baths, lot size)

- Amenities (pool, deck, lakeside view, etc)

- School District

For example, if you're considering purchasing a house that is 1,500 square feet with worn out carpet and old laminated countertops located near a train track and an abandoned building about to collapse, it would NOT be wise to base your value from a home that is 3,000 square feet with nice hardwood floors, granite countertops overlooking a bubbling brook! Needless to say, this would NOT be a similar property and therefore not a comparable sale.

Try to find something that is more similar to what your home will be like after it is all fixed up. The ARV should only be determined from a list of similar Comps that have sold in that area - the operative term being *"that have Sold"*.

Many newbie investors make the mistake of using the tax records to determine the value. Tax records have no bearing on the true value of a home. Current listed prices of houses in a particular area are also not a good basis for comps.

You should always remember that the numbers can only be considered comparable once the properties you're comparing your deal to have already been sold.

FLIP TIP:

Don't base value from available homes for sale or county tax records.

OTHER FACTORS TO CONSIDER

Another key factor in determining if you should move forward on a deal is the <u>DOM</u> or "Days on Market" which shows how long houses in an area typically take to sell.

Neighborhoods that have low DOM, for example, less than 30 days, are typically excellent neighborhoods in which to flip houses. Inversely, areas with very high DOM (4 months+) could be trouble, so stay away from those areas as much as possible.

Essentially, low DOM represents high demand, so finding deals in neighborhoods with low DOM can have a big impact on how quickly your property sells.

DOM should be viewed as a critical piece in your analyzing process, because if you have a property sitting on the market for a long period of time, this translates to high carrying or holding costs.

For example, if you purchase a home for $75,000 and you also borrow $25,000 for repairs, that equals a $100,000 loan/investment cost. If you're financing this with a 12% interest only loan, your payments are going to be roughly $1,000 per month (depending on the total amount that is financed). Don't forget about your property taxes, insurance and utility costs. These carrying costs will definitely eat away at your profits really fast, so moving the property fast is a key ingredient to creating success in the flipping game.

You also want to make sure there aren't a lot of foreclosures in the neighborhood. When an area has a high number of foreclosures, this can severely impact the value of other properties in the neighborhood when appraisals are done. This means that even if you find a qualified buyer for your home, they may not be able to purchase it if the appraisal comes back low because of all of the foreclosures in the neighborhood.

While these neighborhoods can sometimes be good for picking up rental properties for long term wealth building, be weary when finding a 'diamond in the rough' to flip in these neighborhoods.

Another thing to consider is there should NOT be an excessive number of currently listed properties in the neighborhood. When a neighborhood has a lot of homes for sale (inventory), of course, this means there is more competition, and obviously, less demand. This in turn translates to higher DOM and higher holding costs as well.

Here is a review of the Key Points to Analyzing A Deal:

USE THE FORMULA & FREE FLIP ANALYZER

70% of ARV - Minus Repair Costs = Maximum Allowable Offer (MAO)

USE GOOD NUMBERS AND DATA

Be sure you are using accurate comps and similar Comps when determining your property value and sales price.

CONSIDER OTHER FACTORS

Target houses and neighborhoods with low DOM and other appealing features/amenities like school districts and proximity to malls, bus/train stations, main highways etc.

So now that you know how to use the Buying Formula to analyze a deal when it comes your way, let's delve into how you can easily estimate the cost of repairs.

CHAPTER FIVE

ESTIMATING REPAIRS

FLIP FUNDAMENTAL #4 – ESTIMATING REPAIRS

If you follow the action steps from the Deal Flow chapter and begin creating your own source of leads and deals, then you are going to quickly have to learn how to analyze the cost of repairs for these properties. Sadly, I see way too many investors walk away from good deals all of the time because of fear or lack of knowledge about how to estimate repairs. On one hand, this is good, because it allows full time investors like me to swoop in and buy deals that less experienced or 'newbie' investors don't know how to handle. On the other hand, it's unfortunate because with just a bit more education and access to a few simple to use resources, they could have easily been able to determine the cost of those repairs and potentially gone on to make some great profits.

This is definitely a 'make it or break it' section of the book, so grasping the skill of estimating repairs is going to be a determinant to your success or failure. Estimating repairs is a skill indeed, but you need not worry too much because it's a fairly a rather easy one to learn.

The first step is by determining WHAT needs to be repaired.

Going back to the last chapter, you're going to have to keep your Comps in mind when you're estimating the repairs and determining WHAT needs to be done. The WHAT is much more important than the HOW at this point. There is no need to get bogged down by details at this stage in the game. It is more important to make sure you have a close ballpark price on what it's going to cost to perform the necessary repairs.

The key point here is 'NECESSARY REPAIRS'.

Always remember that one of our goals is to closely resemble similar properties that sold quickly in *that* particular market.

So for example, if the comps show that homes in that area had ceramic tile tub surrounds in the bathrooms, then it would be wise to go ahead and factor that into your costs. In other words, don't try to turn your little starter neighborhood flip into a country club palace.

Here is a concept I use to first determine WHAT needs to be done on every project:

- **MUST**

- **SHOULD**

- **WOW**

MUST

MUST items are of course anything that must be done. Basically, these are items that would stop an average potential buyer for that market from buying or making an offer on your home.

These are items you don't even consider not doing. These are items that range from safety or hazard issues, the obvious ones being roofing, foundation, plumbing, electrical issues and the like; to some cosmetic issues such as paint, windows, doors, carpeting, cabinets etc.

For example, if you're buying a home that was built in the 1960's and has not been painted since, of course, a paint job would be a must item. If the home has foundation issues or a worn out leaky roof that is way past its better days, then those would fall into the 'Must' category as well.

SHOULD

A SHOULD item is anything that is 'normal' for that market. This is an area where comps are also quite important. For example, if granite countertops and stainless steel appliances are the standard for that particular neighborhood, then you would be wise to include those into your repair estimate.

These items are different than 'Must' items because you can actually 'get away' without doing some of the 'Should' items and the house would still be presentable.

Be forewarned, if you leave out too many 'Should' items, or if you leave out the critical 'Should' items, you risk deterring potential buyers from making an offer on your property.

Unless you are OK with taking a lower price for your property, you should think twice about leaving out any 'Should' items.

WOW

WOW factors are things like slate tile entrances, frameless shower glass, decks, French doors, etc.

Every home should have at least one or two 'Wow' factors incorporated into the project. These don't necessarily have to be incredibly expensive items, rather just something to set your property apart from the others and to add an additional compelling reason for someone to want to make an offer on your home and a way for you to justify your sales price. A good rule of thumb is to mimic the comps in the neighborhood 'Plus 1'.

'Plus 1' means to add at least one thing that raises the bar. For some neighborhoods, this could be something as simple as installing ceiling fans in all of the bedrooms, or building a small wood deck to the back porch.

Remember, it doesn't have to cost much, but it can create a tremendous amount of 'perceived value' on your potential buyer because you showed attention to detail by adding that 'Plus 1' item to your home.

We'll dig deeper into the aesthetics of the rehab later, but for now I want us to stay focused on estimating the repairs.

So, like I mentioned earlier, when you begin receiving a good amount of deal flow, you're going to have to learn the skill of estimating the cost of repairs. Otherwise, you stand to lose out on a lot of deals.

The first you have to decide what type of estimation you need, which is dependent upon which stage the deal is in:

THE 2 TYPES OF ESTIMATING

Blind Estimate: Blind Estimating is used to quickly analyze a deal before proceeding to invest any further effort, time or money. This can be done without even looking at the deal or even leaving your home for that matter. *This is also sometimes referred to as Quick Estimating.

Accurate Estimate: Accurate Estimating is of course more in depth and done prior to proceeding with a deal and beginning the project. Accurate estimating typically begins the moment you sign the contract and during what is called the 'Option Period'. So, needless to say, more thoroughness and attention to detail will definitely be required here.

We'll discuss the 'Option Period' later in the book.

BLIND ESTIMATE

I like to call this blind estimating because many experienced investors will use this formula before ever seeing a property and because they are often called 'blind' offers when you make an offer on a property without actually seeing the property.

Basically this formula is based off the square footage of a home and the general repair items needed, not including the 'major' components like A/C, Roof & Foundation. I will refer to the A/C, Roof and Foundation as the 'Big 3' moving forward.

Here's a simple to use formula that can help you out with this:

Blind Estimate Formula:

Type or extent of repair Cost per Square Foot

1. Minor patch and paint and new flooring $8.00 - $10.00/sq. ft.

2. Above + Exterior paint and siding repairs, misc. $10.00 - $15.00/sq. ft.

3. Above Items + replacement of plumbing, electrical, kitchen, bathrooms $15.00 - $20.00/sq. ft.

4. Above Items + roof replacement and extensive Exterior repairs $20.00 to $25.00/sq. ft.

After you've selected the category of 1-4 that best suits your property, you'll then want to add in projected cost for the Big 3 Items: A/C, Roof & Foundation.

*The prices we're using in this book are for basic 'Flip Grade' type of repairs and not for Custom/High End remodels and does not include the Big 3 components listed in the previous paragraph. I should also note that construction and material prices vary depending on where you're located in the country and with other factors that cause material and labor prices to decline or rise, which of course, prices are typically rising as we all know.

Now during your course of creating deal flow you will occasionally discover some homes that have been recently updated and may not many repairs. But I will tell you this: A majority of the deals you'll run across will need a lot of repairs. It is for this reason they become "deals" and how we as investors make money, which is by taking on the risk to add the value back into the property. So I like to assume, especially on older homes, that many, if not most, of these repairs will be needed.

Here's another hint: if you think you have found a 'deal' that doesn't need many repairs, there is a good chance: IT'S NOT A DEAL.

This isn't a strict rule written in stone, but more times than not, it is. So proceed with caution because the simple fact is that most 'deals' are deals because they need extensive repairs and investors are usually the only ones that will take on the challenge. The general public usually doesn't see the value that is possible to be added to the property, but we do. That is the difference.

Ok, now during this phase of estimating, you do not want to waste a lot of time or effort. This is just to see if there is even a chance you may have a potential deal.

For example, if a wholesaler calls to tell you about a deal they have, you will usually ask only a few questions and at the same time begin to calculate the blind offer formula in your mind.

Here are a few questions and items you will want to know about:

- How much is the property selling for?

- What is the ARV?

- What condition is the property in?

- What year was it built?

- Square feet

- Roof Conditions

- Foundation Issues

- AC Condition/Age

- General Updating/Condition of the home

Is there anything that makes this property unique? Good or bad? Desirable or Undesirable?

Those are all of the questions/items you will need to know in order to quickly calculate a blind repair cost in your mind.

A couple of the key pieces to keep in mind are the ARV and square footage. The ARV is obvious because the value of the property will affect the cost of the rehab and the type of rehab you perform of course. Homes in the $100k range are less costly to renovate than homes in the $300k range. Square footage is a big factor as well (this is one that many newbie investors fail to recognize) because a 3,000 sq. ft. home will cost *between 30-50%* more to repair as a 1,500 square foot home.

The age of the home is also important because the older the home, generally requires more updating, with items like foundation, roof, electrical, plumbing and A/C that may, most likely, have issues.

Using the aforementioned formula and key elements, after what is generally a five minute discussion with an agent or wholesaler, I will have a general overview of the property. In fact, if I know that particular neighborhood or market, I may even generally make an offer over the phone during the same conversation, or tell them that I don't like the deal, whichever the case may be.

Now, you may be thinking that's ridiculous, right? How can I be serious about making an offer over the phone when I haven't even seen the house yet? What if it's a total dump? What if the agent or wholesaler is not honest with his descriptions? What if this? What if that? Relax. There's a reason for this.

First, let me tell you this is precisely the reason why you should develop a good working relationship with agents or wholesalers. If you do, you'll know that most of the time, they'll come to you with good deals instead of duds. My team of wholesalers and agents are quite familiar with my criteria for deals because we've been working together for quite some time now. You need to strive and work for the same kind of professional relationship.

So, going back to the topic at hand, yes, I'm going to possibly make an offer on the house after only a few minutes of talking with the wholesaler or agent, and even without having seen the property yet. But does this mean I am going to buy the property? Possibly. But since nothing's been put on paper yet, nothing is legally binding at this point.

Here is how I typically make my 'verbal' offer:

"You know, I think these numbers sound really good and I like what I hear so far. I feel comfortable to go ahead and give you a verbal offer of $__ if everything is like you say. I am tied up right now, but I'd like to go by in person tomorrow morning to look at the property and if everything looks like we've discussed, I will sign the contract. Can you give me your word that you will hold it for me until tomorrow morning when I see it in person and verify this information?"

A key thing here is to make sure you let that person know you are intent on moving forward with the deal IF the numbers add up based on the property and it's condition they have presented to you verbally.

So, after that conversation, you would want to run the comps and be prepared to move into the accurate estimating phase to see if everything they've presented really looks good.

Keep in mind the old phrase "Money talks and – y'know what - walks", because this remains true. Just because I've asked the wholesaler or agent to wait until I can look at the property, doesn't mean they absolutely will. It all depends on that individual and the relationship you have with them. You have to keep in mind there are always going to be other investors looking for deals and if they come behind you and put down the earnest money and sign a contract before you get the chance to look at the house, then you have just lost the deal.

Additionally, I must warn you to not get too excited when a wholesaler, realtor or another individual calls you with a potential deal and it sounds like a gold mine. This is especially true if the person bringing you the deal is new to you or your team. Many of the people in our business that bring us deals, tend to exaggerate details from time to time. If they don't exaggerate, sometimes they tend to leave out a few specific details.

So, just understand that in your discussions with agents or wholesalers, you're most likely not receiving *'the truth, the whole truth and nothing but the truth'*, so don't take it personally. Sooner or later, you'll meet people who are fairly consistent in their business dealings with you. These are the people you'll want to add to your team. But until you do, always make it a habit to take agents' and wholesalers' words with a grain or two of salt.

Besides, you don't have to be discouraged when agents or wholesalers exaggerate or leave out certain specific details during your initial conversation with them. I actually like it when they do this, because later when it's time for the actual negotiations, I can use their exaggerations or omissions to get the price down even lower.

Now, allow me to make this process a bit simpler for you.

www.FlipAHouseBook.com/resources

Reference the FreeRehabEstimator on the resources page.

After receiving an endless amount of phone calls from investors asking me how to analyze the costs of repairs, I got wise and created the FreeRehabEstimator website to help everyone out. Aren't I a nice guy?

Gee thanks, I'm blushing. :-)

In all seriousness, estimating the cost of repairs is a serious issue, and not to be taken lightly, so make sure you use caution during this phase of your due diligence.

The FreeRehabEstimator is a comprehensive rehab list that allows you to simply fill in each item, line by line, to come up with your repair estimate. Of course there are several types of software and websites like this, so feel free to search around for the one that you like best, but since this is the one I created and use, I think we'll just stick with this one for the purposes of the book.

I tried to make the Blind/Quick repair estimation process as simple as possible with the FreeRehabEstimator.com software by creating a spreadsheet (alphabetized) you can follow line by line.

I know, some of the pricing on the FreeRehabEstimator is not going to be exact and some of these items will vary depending upon your geographical location and cost of materials. However, it can still give you a close enough approximation and help you decide on whether or not to sign a contract on the property and move into the contract phase which will lead you to also Accurate Estimating of the repairs.

If you don't know an exact cost, or if you run into an item that is not on the Free Rehab Estimator, simply 'guesstimate' on those items (input them in the last section, 'Miscellaneous') until you can determine more solid numbers.

As you gain more experience rehabbing homes, pricing will become much easier for you to pin point. For the items you're unsure about, many of these prices can be determined by a quick phone call or Internet search.

Just a reminder, the FreeRehabEstimator is only intended to give you a quick, general idea of the cost of repairs and not intended to be 100% accurate.

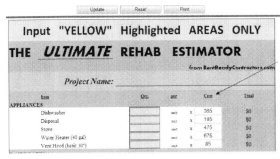

Note: Because construction costs can fluctuate and vary widely depending on geographical location, we made the 'Cost' column so you can adjust pricing on the FreeRehabEstimator. Now you can increase/decrease pricing based on the costs of your region. Always be sure to adjust pricing according to your local market because price will vary depending on your specific location.

Another good rule of thumb is after you have calculated all of your projected costs; throw another 10% on top, JUST IN CASE. You will be wiser for doing this.

Lastly, NEVER leave a necessary repair or line item blank just because you don't know exact cost. Be sure you include a price for every item of work that is needed for the property. If you don't know the exact price, it doesn't matter, just make a 'guesstimate' on what you think it will be. This doesn't mean take a wild, random guess. It means to take an educated guess. You can go about this by 'Googling' it so you can determine a rough price of repairs for items you are unfamiliar with.

The bottom line with estimating repairs is that it is far more important to be comprehensive, than it is to be precisely accurate.

What I'm talking about, is if you think a flip house needs a new roof, it's better to estimate it at $5,000 than to leave it off because you're unsure of pricing. If it ends up costing $6,000 your "educated guesstimate" of $5,000 is much closer than $0. On the other hand, if the actual bid comes in less, the difference automatically gets chalked up to your profits.

For some of the more technical items, like A/C, Roof or foundation repair, you will need to call a local service company to provide an estimate, which leads me to the second type of Estimating, which is ACCURATE ESTIMATING.

ACCURATE ESTIMATING

This is the next level of estimating and this is where you're going to have to roll up your sleeves a bit and understand that your actions here are one of the keys that separates the losers from winners, so you'll need to stay focused as we dive into this. Don't worry and don't be scared.

I can assure you that this phase of estimating is not going to be that difficult nor is it going to be something that conjures up nightmares, but there is some work involved. This process is actually quite simple easy once you get the hang of it. Just keep in mind that these estimates are what are going to make your piece of the pie either bigger or smaller. So the more clarity you have on how to do this, the better job you'll do and the bigger your piece of the action will be.

Basically, I can sum up how to achieve Accurate Estimates in one sentence:

Accurate Estimates can only be achieved by obtaining estimates from legitimate Contractors and Trades.

Written estimates are always going to be preferred over verbal, but if the Contractor or Trades person you're dealing with is reputable, a verbal price is acceptable in certain situations.

The tricky part is finding the contractors to provide the estimates and how to do this quickly. The best way to find a list of contractors is from your local real estate investment clubs, fellow real estate investors, periodicals and the local better business bureau. Your local wholesalers and hard money lenders can also refer you to some good contractors. I want to reinforce and strongly encourage you try your best to work with Contractors and Trades that have verifiable references and a proven track record. Yes, you may occasionally have to look online, or in the local paper, but it's always best to find people to work with that have a few solid references from other investors.

Generally, Contractors are more than happy to provide quotes on a property that you're under contract to purchase because it means they have a legitimate opportunity to earn your business. However, if you don't already own the property nor do you have the property under contract for purchase, you should let the service provider/contractor know this upfront. Obviously, contractors and service companies do not like to waste their time on providing estimates if they do not have a reasonable chance of earning the business. So be respectful of their time and gas money. We rarely ask Contractors to provide estimates for properties that we don't own or have under contract.

Yes, you can ask them to provide bids for homes you don't have under contract, and they may do this a time or two, but if you're serious about building a legitimate investing business that is built to last, it's critical that you create strong working relationships with your contractors. Trust me, you can burn bridges very quickly by not respecting people's time. However, you can ask if they can give you a 'rough estimate' over the phone, or offer a small fee for them to provide an estimate.

I recommend having a list of repairs you can give to general contractors to bid on so you can initially assess them as well as gain insight from their expertise. You may want to consider not telling them every single thing you want done because by allowing some things off, you can see what their recommendations are and get a sense of their experience and attention to detail.

The bottom line for Accurate Estimating once again is this:

Accurate Estimates can only be achieved by obtaining estimates from legitimate Contractors and Trades.

So as long as you doing your part to find trusted Contractors and Trades and making sure you are being comprehensive in building your scope of work and obtaining accurate pricing for all the work that needs to be done, then you'll be just fine.

Lastly, like I mentioned in the Blind/Quick estimating section, always by sure to 'pad' your rehab budgets because more times than not, rehab budgets will go over. Generally, 10% is a good number to add to your budget for unforeseen items that often times, will appear.

Here is a review of the Key Points to Estimating Repairs:

MUST - SHOULD - WOW

First determine what MUST be done to make the property safe and stable, then determine what SHOULD be done to make the property marketable, lastly add in 1-2 WOW factors to ensure the home sells quickly and is a step above your competition.

BLIND/QUICK ESTIMATING

Learn to quickly analyze a deal before proceeding to invest any further effort or time, this can often be done simply based off current pictures of the home.

ACCURATE ESTIMATING

This is more in depth, extensive, repair estimating and requires obtaining estimates from legitimate Contractors and Trades.

CHAPTER SIX

GOING UNDER CONTRACT

Before discussing some of the aspects of going under contact on a property, I'd first like to talk a little about negotiations that precede the contract phase. Based on my own experience in this business, generally speaking, hardcore negotiating is not required when trying to score a deal.

While other investors would say negotiating savvy is a top requirement when securing a deal, I strongly disagree. For people who believe negotiation is not really their cup of tea, you can let out a sigh of relief now. I'm telling you, if you follow my method and approach, you won't feel the need for hardcore negotiating.

So first, let me ask you a question: Have you ever seen an ugly baby?

Well I have.

Do you think when I saw that baby I told the parents their baby was cosmetically challenged?

Of course not!

Besides, who's to say an ugly baby can't grow up to be a beautiful person right?

Just to state the obvious, it would not have been polite nor would it have done any good to let someone know their baby is ugly.

The same thing goes with someone's house. Just because a house is 'ugly' - and believe me, you'll come across many of them that are very ugly - doesn't mean you need to come right out and tell the owner their house is a messed up pile of bricks and sticks!

Unfortunately, I see a lot of investors do this, they will make it their main goal to reinforce over and over to the homeowner, agent or wholesaler the house is the most horrible thing in the neighborhood just so they can try to get a lower price.

For one thing, this is rude. Second, I've found that it's not very effective. Third, most of these people know their home is in need of serious repair. They just don't know how to get out of the situation they are in. You're just courting disaster if you go right out and tell them their house is downright ugly without first establishing a relationship first.

"You will attract more bees with honey than vinegar."

If you're dealing directly with a seller, many times, you're dealing with families in difficult situations. Loss of job, loss of a loved one, sickness, disability and the list goes on and on. Of course, every one's situation is different, but I strongly recommend to always be sensitive towards their plight, without becoming emotionally involved, since your interest is mainly business. And please remember during the lesson on deal flow, this is a job in my opinion that I would prefer to be left to Realtors and wholesalers to deal with and not something we as investors want to do very often, but for those of you doing your own direct marketing, yes, you will be dealing one-on-one with people in all kinds of difficult situations, so you'll need to be prepared.

I think the 'Treat others as you want to be treated' rule fares well here to say the least. You'll find people will respond better if you are respectful, honest and 'diplomatic', that is, not using 'brutal truth' as your approach.

Besides, we as investors are only going to pay what the house is worth (remember the formula), so work your numbers and offer the amount that makes the deal attractive to you and work with the people who are looking to sell within your buying parameters.

Let me tell you a quick personal story to drive this point home.

When I was twelve, my family fell on hard times for a couple of years. My parents ended up falling behind on mortgage payments among other things and the rest is history. We lost our house and a lot more. The house was actually bought by a real estate investor right before we were foreclosed on, much like I do today. Ironic, huh?

When my family lost our home, it was tough, but so is life. My parents really had no choice based on some blows life was dealing at the time. And the investor wasn't a bad guy for seizing an opportunity from someone else's hard times. Remember, in every crisis there is an opportunity. I'm sure the investor profited from buying our home. On the other hand, my family avoided having a foreclosure on their credit and rebounded nicely from the whole experience a few years later. So in a way, both sides benefited from the sale.

The way I see it is this, a home is an investment, much like stocks. Some people decide, due to various circumstances, to sell their investment at a discounted price (some even choosing to take huge losses) in order to avoid even greater losses had they decided to hold on to their investment (like having a foreclosure in your credit history).

However, the market always determines the price and no one is forcing them to accept any offer. Like I said, if a seller doesn't accept my offer, that's fine with me, I will wish them the best of luck and I'll simply move on to the next one.

I know what it takes to be profitable in this business so I have to hold true to my numbers, because at the end of the day, I have a business to run and a family to provide for. This means I can never "afford" to overpay on a property just because someone is in a difficult situation. I just won't do it, and neither should you. Besides all of that, I will be the first to admit that I'm not a big negotiator.

This is another reason I primarily like working with wholesalers, because generally, their price is firm and I can simply make a decision on the deal, whether to go directly into contract or pass on the deal.

Does this mean that I never negotiate with sellers or wholesalers? Absolutely not. There are many times I negotiate deals, but I do utilize a few guidelines and it's not something I do routinely on every deal 'as a rule'.

Some investors (especially newbies) feel like they're supposed to be a hard ball negotiator on every deal they do and really beat the seller, agent or wholesaler up to squeeze out every last nickel. What they're most likely really doing is thwarting a good relationship and lessening the likelihood of that person ever calling them back when they have another deal.

I come more from the school of "speak softly and carry a big stick" philosophy, with the 'stick' referring to cash combined with a firm offer. Let me explain. I have found there are a lot of 'flakes' in this business. Because of this, I've always conducted myself in such a way as to make sure I always keep my word. "I say what I'll do and I'll do what I say". Most often times, rather than negotiate, I will make my offer, let the seller know that I will close fast with cash and assure them they won't have to worry about me backing out, and that usually does the trick. Of course, I will always make them aware the only reason I would back out is if there was some unforeseen issue with the house that was not disclosed or uncovered. This puts the ball back in their court.

I've found when a seller trusts and likes the buyer, they will even accept less for their property. This may sound strange, but it's very true. I recently bought a home from a wholesaler friend of mine in which the seller sold it to my friend for $20,000 less than another offer. And the reason was simply because they liked him better than the other guys there were talking with. Go figure. :-)

Whether you're the one negotiating the deal or not, always remember, EVERYTHING COMES DOWN TO THE NUMBERS.

If the numbers make sense, go ahead and do the deal. If they don't add up, pass. It's as simple as that.

Besides, generally speaking, since a majority of my deal flow comes directly from wholesalers, there isn't always a lot of room to negotiate. Now, don't get me wrong, there are still some opportunities to 'adjust' pricing in various ways. And I do occasionally seize those opportunities. But that's more of the exception than the rule so I recommend you steer clear of that scenario unless you're really comfortable you can pull it off.

Here's a simple, but effective strategy I use to immediately win the wholesalers to my side:

OFFER FULL PRICE

I know, some of you are scratching your heads, because you've read in some other book or some boot camp to offer 18.67% lower than asking price or some other magical equation.

Sorry, but it really doesn't work that way. Let me explain why I may decide to offer full price, even if it is slightly above my Maximum Allowable Offer:

1. A full price offer is most likely to get accepted.

2. If I lowball them with my price, then the seller is less likely to accept my offer, and I have subsequently wasted my time and my agent's time.

3. If the repairs are going to be more than projected, I can back out of the deal or renegotiate it.

4. If I offer them their asking price, they are starting to see dollar signs!

Did you see the significance of the last reason? When I go under contract on a property, the seller gets excited because they are one step closer to getting paid. I am the hero here because if I proceed with the contract they get paid and I get the house.

Now let's discuss a bit more in depth about going into the Contract phase without creating additional work for yourself.

CONTRACTS

A lot of investors spend a lot of time studying forms, contracts and other real estate paperwork and processes. I think it is great to learn and to educate yourself in any trade or investment venture that you enjoy and are serious about. However, just because you've read a real estate book doesn't make you a real estate agent.

Therefore, I will tell you that even though I have a real estate license, even I use a licensed real estate agent to write most of my offers and contracts. Just the same as I always use a title company to close on properties and I always use an attorney to draw up any legal documents.

Could I do some of these things myself? Of course I could, but I never will. The main reason why is because it's not my trade or background. I could make a mistake that could cost me big time. Secondly, please remember the goal of this book is for you to become a successful house flipper while working less. This goes back to making up your mind to be a real estate investor, not a document preparer or admin assistant.

So please, outsource all of these responsibilities to professionals who specialize in these areas. Now, lets look at what is needed to officially make an offer.

5 Components of an Offer

1. Purchase Price

2. Earnest Money

3. Closing Costs

4. Closing Date

5. Acceptance Date

Even when a contract is signed by both the seller and buyer and earnest money and an option fee has been paid, this doesn't guarantee that the buyer has to buy the property. The buyer should still have an 'Exit Clause' included in a properly constructed contract and use of the **"Option Period"**.

So what is the 'Option Period'? An Option Period is a provisional period on a contract that allows the buyer to have a certain number of days to "opt out" of the contract and only lose the "option fee" but not their earnest money.

In most states, the option fee can range from as little as $10 to $100 or even more depending on the buyer. I typically keep mine at only $10. There is no set fee or number of days for the option period. In my home market of Texas, the option period usually ranges 7-10 days for around $100 option fee.

During the option period, which we also refer to as your due diligence phase, you can begin to inspect the property and begin to get estimates from contractors. This may also be the best time for you to actually go out and check the property in person.

It is imperative and extremely important that you begin performing your due diligence immediately. There are 2 persons from whom you can get vital information during this stage:

1. Home Inspectors

2. Contractors

HOME INSPECTORS

Many investors will pay a professional home inspector to come out during this option period. A home inspector will inspect the entire property including foundation, HVAC, roof, plumbing (basic), electrical, etc. Typically, home inspection reports range from $250 - $650. They will provide a detailed report showing all of the potential 'issues' that may need to be repaired.

Quick note: Just because a home inspector notates something on their report, it doesn't mean it must necessarily be repaired. For example, there are many items on a home inspectors report that are new code issues and not necessarily required for older homes. A lot of times the home will be 'grandfathered' in on many of these older existing issues. It's best to ask your local home inspector or contractor to determine which issues are 'must dos'.

I should also note that if you pay for a home inspector to prepare a written report, you must disclose this report to the potential homebuyers when you enter into the contract phase with them. When a potential buyer sees this report (especially a first time homebuyer), they can really get scared off from buying the home after seeing what the home was really like before you worked on it. This may not be a huge issue if you did a complete gut job renovation, but if you just did a 'paint and carpet' type rehab and left many of those old issues unresolved from the inspection report, you may be putting yourself in jeopardy of losing your buyer. Your potential buyers may have significant fear now that you cut a lot of corners and they may be unwilling to move forward on purchasing your home at this point.

One strategy that I have seen house flippers take is to pay a home inspector a fee (about half of the normal inspection fee) to do a walk-through of the property to discuss all of the issues but NOT write up a formal report. This is essentially paying for a consultation, rather a full report documented inspection. There are several advantages to this approach:

1. This is a great educational experience for new investors

2. This prevents you from having to disclose a report to the buyers when it comes time for you to sell the property

3. It allows you to address any 'big' issues prior to listing the property on the market and decide what issues you do not need to repair.

CONTRACTORS

When working with Contractors during this option period, the key is to obtain Accurate bids like we discussed during the previous chapter for the repairs that will be needed for the property so you can make sure the total cost of repairs is in line with your anticipated rehab numbers.

It's always best if you can obtain at least 3 written bids from general contractors that come from recommended sources. Prior to this point you should already have some general contracting companies in mind that you would want to use and just as important, contact the contractors the first day you go under contract so that you will be sure to get the bids back before the end of the option period.

The main goal during this phase is to gain as much information as possible about all of the needed repairs and determine if the costs are in line with what you anticipated. However, don't back out of a deal ONLY because the home inspector or contractors uncover additional issues of the house that you weren't aware of. Your first action should be to use these findings as a negotiating tool to get the seller to lower their price.

For me, going into the Option Period and 'negotiations' go hand in hand, because the negotiations may actually 'reignite' or sometimes only begin at the exact moment the contract is signed.

Let me explain:

Many times, if the numbers appear 'good' from the beginning, I really don't negotiate at all and I will sign the contract immediately and proceed with closing as planned. As I said before, I don't like wasting time, mine or others, with super low ball offers and throwing out offers all over the place. So the only offers I make are numbers that I know I like. If they accept my offer, fine, let's sign a contract. And if they don't accept my original offer, fine, on to the next one.

I use the option period to really dig into the deal and start looking at what repairs are really needed to get this ugly duckling to the beauty pageant. During this period, if we uncover any major issues that need to be addressed, I take note of these and use them as leverage to either have the seller take care of the 'newly discovered' issues, renegotiate the price, or to simply execute the option and get out of the contract.

You can have your agent prepare an amendment requesting the seller to repair the specific items that need to be addressed, which for the record I don't recommend. This doesn't mean the seller has to make the repairs you've requested. Oftentimes, this simply opens up the door for a renegotiation of the price, which is what we ultimately want out of this situation, which is a lower purchase price.

However, if the seller refuses to make the required repairs or re-negotiate the contract, you can then "execute the option" and terminate the contract right there on the spot. No questions asked. You'll receive your earnest money back if you do this before the option period expires. The seller would be able to keep the option fee. That's okay since it's generally only going to be a small amount.

Most often, the seller will agree to lower their price or make some concessions on the deal. As a rule, like I briefly mentioned earlier, you should almost never allow the seller to actually have the 'newly discovered' repairs done. Instead you will want your own contractors to do the work after you own the home.

You can almost always negotiate a significantly lower price on the contract using newly discovered repairs as leverage, and have your own contractors do the repair at a lower amount (since they're already working on the deal with you anyway). The difference and savings will show up as additional profits of course.

My only goal during this "due diligence phase" is to get the seller to lower their price. But only if I find additional repairs that are grossly beyond my initial expectations. To be clear I'm not talking about minor repair items, the only thing I really care about are the major components and excessive costs that severely affect the profitability of the deal.

Always document your findings from general contractors and home inspectors as this can become invaluable and really help you to get the price down. I know some investors that use this repair negotiating technique on every deal and go under contract with the intent to dishonestly 'scare' the seller with an overblown cost of repairs or some other issue to try to get them to come way down on their price.

To be honest, of course I'm absolutely trying to get a great deal every time I buy a home, but keep in mind, 'What goes around comes around' so when I go back to renegotiate the deal I come equipped with verified facts and I mean business.

I'll share an example of a conversation between myself and a homeowner that I have a contract with to purchase their home. Let's assume that this home would be worth $100,000 after it was repaired. I believe it needs approximately $15,000 in repairs and I am under contract to purchase it for $55,000:

Me: "Mr./Mrs. House Seller, I really like your home, it's got a great backyard and I love what you've done with the master bath shower. Was that layout the original design?"

(I always start with some positive remarks about the house. Believe me, this isn't always easy to do, because some of these houses are messed up! But this is a MUST for negotiations.)

Mr./Mrs. House Seller: "Well thanks, no, we reconfigured that bathroom back in 1983. It was a lot of work, but luckily my cousin's a handyman plumber, so he helped out and it wasn't too bad."

Me: "It's good to have help when tackling projects like that. Now, Mr./Mrs. House Seller, I did notice that the house, unfortunately, has some other issues that I wasn't aware of when we first signed the contract. For example, it looks like the foundation is showing signs of settlement and the roof is also going to need to be replaced."

Mr./Mrs. House Seller: "Yes sir, we've been meaning to get the roof done, we just haven't had the money to do it. And the foundation issues have really become more noticeable lately."

Me: "Well, I know we have a contract for $59,000, but after learning about these repairs that your house needs, unfortunately, in order to go forward, we'll have to reduce the price to about $41,000. Is this something that you're in position to do? If not, I totally understand."

Mr./Mrs. House Seller: "Whoa! Wait a minute, we have to reduce the price by that much?"

Me: "Well, unfortunately, there are additional items my contractor found. It looks like the water heater is bad and the entire HVAC system is beyond repair and will need replacement. Due to these unforeseen expenses, that would be the most I will be able to offer for this home."

The goal here is to politely, let the seller know that their house is in need of more repairs than they originally thought. Remember we don't want to list every little item, just a few of the major costs. And you should always come from a place of caring and empathy. You are there to take the burden off their hands because usually these are things they cannot or do not want to do themselves.

Mr./Mrs. House Seller: "I know you're right about the repairs, I just wasn't expecting to lower the price that much. I was really hoping to get the full price of $59,000, but to be honest, I am fed up with this house, and I'm just ready to get rid of it and move on."

Me: "I understand, I will contact my agent and have her amend the contract so we can move closer to the closing."

Now, let's talk about the dynamics of what took place in this brief conversation. First, let me say that if the house only needed $15,000 in repairs, I had every intention to move forward with the deal and purchase the property. So, by that, I am going into contract with the seller with good intentions.

Second point, this conversation likely would have never taken place if I hadn't given them the full price offer to begin with. If I had low-balled them in the beginning, then they probably would not have accepted my offer. Instead, I gave them the asking price and was able to establish a rapport with them. That, in turn, led to this conversation.

Just as important, I typically start the conversation off with some positive remarks. If for some reason I can't find anything nice to say about the house (which happens on occasion) I will start off saying something positive about something, maybe their pet, or car or anything! Then, as the conversation progresses, you want to respectfully bring to their attention the unforeseen needed repairs that were discovered after you went under contract. Make sure to phrase it in such a way that reminds them these repairs will be their responsibility if they don't sell the house to you. This reminds them about the 'pain' of the situation, which will often times remind them to stay focused on selling the home rather than having to deal with the issues the property has.

When you find yourself in a similar position as this, be prepared to walk away from the deal if the seller isn't willing to come down to the numbers that work. No worries, you can move on to the next one because there are always plenty of fish in the sea.

During the negotiating phase, there is a definite psychological element at play and you need to be aware of it at all times. It is the "Pleasure-Pain" principle. Here's how it works: People gravitate towards pleasure and avoid pain. With that being said, you want to represent 'Pleasure' in your conversation in the sense you can be the person that can take this 'Pain' (house and repairs) off their hands and head.

So, once again, I try to mention the large repairs that are needed without adding too much insult to injury. The more you can respectfully incorporate gentle reminders of all of the improvements they would need to perform in order to sell their home for retail value, the more you'll be able to induce the seller to become more motivated to just be done with the property and sell it at a discount.

Like I said before, these negotiation techniques primarily work when I'm dealing directly with sellers and these negotiating strategies don't necessarily apply to offers I make on big bank-owned properties and some of the deals that are brought to me by wholesalers. The same will be true for you.

If I like the numbers from them, I will go with the deal, no haggling required. For some bank owned properties, I may offer a lower price than their listed price because I know that banks aren't typically going to get into a big negotiation with me. So I will submit an offer that makes my numbers work and go from there.

In regards to wholesalers I work with, the same thing goes, typically they are not going to bring a deal to me if the numbers aren't good, so there is usually not much negotiating involved. If there is a deal that I'm not that crazy about, I will ask them if they can lower their price to my "sweet spot" where I would really like to see the deal at. If they can't do it, I will walk away from the deal. I try not to haggle too much with my team of wholesalers because I know if I become too big of a hassle, they'll simply begin to take their deals to other investors. That being said, if they are not bringing me good deals, or they're getting greedy with their assignment fees, I will let them know right up front.

I try to create a real team atmosphere with everyone that I do business with. This has proven to be a really powerful strategy and it has allowed me to establish great relationships built on trust and transparency. Not to mention, it makes business transactions go much smoother. In a nutshell, this is how I see the entire process of making a decision to ink a deal:

When it comes to deciding on buying a house to flip, the numbers have to be great. I mean, I need to feel like I want to jump out of my chair and do a back flip. If the deal doesn't get me really excited then I will not do it.

Now I hope you are beginning to see why creating deal flow is so important. If you have a lot deals coming your way, then it becomes very easy to "Just Say No". It gives you the ability to cherry pick the really good ones and let the others fall to the wayside.

This is another reason why I don't waste a lot of time negotiating. I simply let my team bring me their best deals because they know if they bring me a really good one, I will buy it and close quickly with cash.

So, you may be wondering how I can close quickly with cash right? We'll talk about that in the next chapter, but first let's take a quick review of what we learned in this section.

Here is a review of the Key Points to Negotiations, Contracts & Inspections

NEGOTIATIONS

- Don't waste your time throwing out low ball offers all over the place. Make offers based on solid numbers that you feel great about.

- Generally offer full price if you like the numbers, then renegotiate the deal if you discover additional major repairs that are needed during the option period.

CONTRACTS

- Always use a professional to help with any paperwork involved in the deal to satisfy the 5 Components of an Offer/Contract.

INSPECTIONS

- You should almost never get an official inspection on a home you intend to flip because you will always have to disclose the report when you're getting ready to sell the home.

- At the most, you should have an inspector that you trust do consulting walk through with you.

CHAPTER SEVEN

FINANCING

FLIP FUNDAMENTAL #5 – FINANCING

Perhaps the most overused excuse given for people failing to invest in Real Estate is, *"I can't invest in Real Estate because I don't have any money"*. *I'm* sorry, but you'll have to leave your excuses behind if you want to achieve success in this business. If you're like many and a lack of funds is your personal excuse for not flipping, allow me to be the one to break it to you, it's a LOUSY EXCUSE!

I realize that many of you reading this are like me when I started out and you don't even have 2 nickels to rub together. I know. I've been there and I've done that. It's difficult, I get it. It's all the more reason for you to square up and do your first flip - FAST. Don't lose faith my friend. There is a light at the end of the tunnel.

We discussed earlier about using OPT (Other People's Time with agents and wholesalers), well now you're going to learn how to use OPM, Other People's Money.

In today's market, you must know how to wisely use leverage to fund your deals. And the cash you use doesn't necessarily have to be your own. Especially if you're like me when I started - broke as a joke.

Let's face reality. In today's economy, we are in a time and country where our government is printing money almost non-stop thus causing entrepreneurs to adjust to the market conditions continuously. This means you must be smart when funding your deals.

Do you think Donald Trump uses his own money when he does a real estate transaction? Absolutely not. He does what any intelligent entrepreneur would do. He simply raises the capital to fund the deal, which is what we call Leverage.

Raising capital is the #1 skill an entrepreneur needs to have in his arsenal. And just like all other skills, it can be learned. The good news about this skill is it's easier to acquire than you think.

Just trust me on this: There's plenty of money around. In fact, money abounds. But, in this business, money is NOT what you need most.

Let me repeat this statement:

Money is NOT what you need most!

Creative Thinking is what you need.

Real estate is not like conventional investments like stocks, mutual funds, CD's and the like where you literally need to have and own the money you're going to invest. Real estate allows you to be creative and structure deals in a number of different ways where you don't have to use your own money for your deals if you choose not to. You just need to find a creative way to do it. In essence, if you have the will, there is a way.

Am I saying that you should not use your own cash to invest if you have it available? No, that is not what I'm saying. Now that I'm at a place in my life that I have capital to invest, real estate is the only place that I invest my money. However, for this book, I'm going to show you ways that are possible to structure deals creatively so you have options on whether or not to use your own cash in your deals. A lot of times, it is easier to use some of your own cash, but combine with another source of financing, which we will soon discuss.

Let's discuss the most popular financing options to fund your flip:

1.   Banks

2.   Hard Money

3.   Cash

4.   Partnerships

5.   Private Money

BANKS

Yes, Bank loans are still available in today's market, but this type of financing is much more difficult to obtain than it was a few years ago.

Today's banks are looking for individuals with superb credit scores and lots of cash in the bank. If you are able to get long-term bank financing with low interest rates, I highly recommend you take advantage of this financing to add high yield cash-flow rental properties to your portfolio for long term wealth building.

However, when it comes to quick flips, this is not generally considered a viable option. Why?

Banks are extremely slow, require tons of paperwork, typically require lots of money down and typically won't lend on a property in need of repairs. Besides that, in today's market, they generally require down payments of up to 20% and you do not have the option of closing quickly.

One possibility to utilize banks for your flips is by having a bank line of credit. Some investors have established relationships with local banks that will extend them lines of credit they use to purchase homes. These credit lines generally come with a 4-8% interest rates and with only minimal fees involved. We've utilized a line of credit for years and almost always have this capital at work on our deals. So, if you have access to lines of credit, this would be considered a very viable and recommended source of financing for your deals. Otherwise, I strongly recommend looking elsewhere for financing your flips.

HARD MONEY

Hard Money loans are the types of loans I used when I first began buying houses. They are probably the most common form of financing for investors flipping homes.

Basically, hard money loans are high-interest loans (generally between 12-15%) given to real estate investors for properties in need of repair.

The main advantage of a hard money loan is they are from 'asset based' lenders so they are willing to make a loan on a house that is in need of repair and they are not as concerned with the borrower's credit score, assets and income like typical banks are.

Another benefit of working with a hard money lender is they will act as a 'safeguard' if you are uncertain about the numbers of a deal. For example, hard money lenders typically use a similar formula that we learned earlier, 70% ARV - Minus Repair Costs = Maximum Loan Amount, when determining if the loan 'makes sense'. This is because hard money lenders, generally, only lend on deals where they can be sure they'll get their money back plus interest. Therefore, if a hard money lender analyzes your deal and refuses to lend you the money to buy the house, that can be a strong 'Warning Flag' for you to go find another deal.

Another advantage of working with hard money lenders is they will also lend you the money for repairs. Typically, the way this process works is you will initially have to complete these repairs before they will release this money to you. In other words, after you pay for the repairs out of pocket, they will reimburse you the cost of repairs after all of the repairs have been completed.

The repairs do not have to be 100% complete before you can get reimbursed, it can be set up in multiple draws (1-3 typically) after certain items are complete. For example, if you were replacing the roof, and the hard money lender had $4,000 set aside for that repair, once the roofing work is complete, you could call for a draw inspection of the roof and the lender would release a check to you for the $4,000 that was budgeted in for the roof.

However, while there are a lot of advantages in using hard money for your deals, I need to inform you of some of the details about it:

- Interest rates typically range from 12-15%

- 1-4 points are charged to originate the loan (a point is 1% of the total loan amount)

- A down payment and monthly payments are required (not ideal for cash flow)

- These are generally short term loans (6-12 months)

- Repair funds are only released as work is completed

- Repair Inspections typically cost $100-150 per occurrence

- I know you may be thinking these terms are somewhat 'hard' to swallow.

Well, now you know why it is called HARD money.

That being said, I've seen a lot of investors balk at hard money lenders' terms and walk away from a good deal just because they think it is too expensive. I have to disagree with that attitude.

If the numbers work on your deal by using hard money loans, I would recommend you definitely consider this option. I have been able to make a lot of money on real estate deals that have been financed with hard money loans.

When I used hard money loans in the past, I just considered the higher interest rates and points as the cost of doing business. It's like I'm attending a really good business school (some call it the School of Hard Knocks, but if you do it right, you can dodge most, if not all, the knocks you get dealt with) and this is simply my tuition. But unlike any normal school and tuition, I know for sure I'm learning and developing the skillsets needed to becoming a great entrepreneur.

I encourage new investors to get to know some of the local hard money lenders and familiarize themselves with their loan terms and processes. This is so when you find a deal, you will be ready to move forward with it.

Working with hard money lenders is similar to working with contractors, in that you should meet with several different ones before selecting who you're going to work with. Make sure you know up front, in writing, what the terms and conditions are.

Every hard money lender will have a different set of guidelines and terms, so make sure you're in full understanding of all of these conditions and make sure it is a company you will be able to work well with.

A good hard money lender is a critical piece to building a successful team for your business, especially when you are first starting out so begin seeking out a hard money lender to add to your team.

CASH

Utilizing cash can be a great advantage when you're writing offers to purchase homes, because if you have cash it shows you are a serious buyer and can close quickly. There is no doubt about it, when you can put on the contract that you can close quickly with cash, it will help you get more offers accepted.

Additionally, it often allows you to negotiate a better deal on the property because sellers are willing to accept less for their property if you have cash. This is because they feel more confident you can close and close sooner than someone going through the bank loan process.

Let me reinforce the last sentence:

SELLERS ARE WILLING TO ACCEPT LESS FOR THEIR PROPERTY IF YOU CAN CLOSE WITH CASH.

That can be a huge advantage for real estate investors getting contracts accepted, and at lower prices than your competitors. Yes, I understand most people don't have enough cash to purchase and rehab a home. I was no different when I started investing in Real Estate. When I first got started, as you know, I had zero cash. But for those of you who do have the capital to do so, let's discuss a little further.

We already mentioned that when you close with cash you can close quickly and usually negotiate a lower purchase price. These are undoubtedly huge advantages. However, if you decide to use your own cash to purchase houses you have to realize, every one's cash is limited at some point. So if you plan on doing multiple deals, you are going to severely limit yourself at some point in time if you don't have access to other forms of financing.

Additionally, you must consider that if anything were to happen to the house (fire, acts of God, etc.), or if there is a substantial market shift and you can't sell your home according to your original time-frame, your money may be tied up for a very long time before it gets reimbursed.

Furthermore, if you, God forbid, get into some 'life event' that requires extra money (medical conditions, job lay off, etc.) and your cash is tied up in the house until it sells, then this could cause some undue stress for sure.

While the term "Cash Is King" still applies, it would be better stated as, "He Who Has Access To Cash Is King" as I'll explain this statement later when we discuss Private Money. So if you are flush with cash, this is an option to finance your flips, albeit, with some considerations before proceeding forward.

PARTNERSHIPS

So, why would you consider partnering with somebody on a flip?

Well, one of the main reasons you may see partnering on a deal as a viable option is simply because you don't have a way to finance a deal by yourself. Maybe you're like me when I got started - with zero cash. It may even be worse for you and not only do you not have any cash, you may also have poor credit. Well, like I said earlier, when there is a will, there will always be a way and sometimes partnering on a deal becomes the way for you to make it happen.

Basically, when you partner on a deal, what you're really doing is creatively making something happen that wouldn't or couldn't happen by yourself alone. This is another key ingredient to successful entrepreneurs - creatively making things happen when others would simply give up.

For example, let's say you have a friend who has the cash or credit available needed to finance a flip and they like the idea of investing in real estate. One option is to form a partnership or joint venture agreement with that person so they can provide the financing on the deal and you would essentially take care of all other aspects of the deal.

Your profits could be significantly lower when partnering, and even possibly cut in half (depending on your partnership agreement) than if you did the deal yourself, but consider this: If you partner with someone who is putting up all of the cash to fund the deal, you personally have ZERO holding costs, points, etc. This means you have ZERO cash input but you get to keep 50% of the profit. You're practically making money out of thin air! Besides, without this partner you may not have been able to close the deal at all and it would be your profits that will be ZERO.

I have consistently been able to earn great returns for my partners' investments in my deals. As a result, I rarely see myself in a situation where I'm at a loss where to get funding for my deals. My partners practically beg me to take their money and invest it because they know they'll get good returns out of my deals. This should be your goal too.

I don't mind sharing the profits on my partnership deals, I actually enjoy that as much as keeping it all for myself. You see, people in our country have been devastated in the stock market recently and because of this I feel like I have been given an opportunity to help these people recoup some of their hard earned money. I take a lot of pride in this. You see, I see my real estate investing business as my morale duty and obligation as a way to serve my community and my investors and partners.

Furthermore, it essentially allows me to do an unlimited number of deals because while I may at times be limited in my own finances or resources, the number of partners available is virtually limitless. This same opportunity is available for you when you put together profitable flip deals for your network of partners.

Now, before I get too carried away here, let me remind you that you should be VERY selective on the individuals that you partner with. Always be on the lookout for people whom you can develop a long-term business relationship with.

Another important thing to remember is that since you are the real estate investor, you should try to remain in control of the decision making on the real estate stuff. After all, this is going to be your 'profession' so you should exercise some sort of authority when it comes to real estate matters. Always be clear on this right from the get go: they put up the money, you take care of the deal and you both share the take at whatever split you agree upon.

There is tremendous value in finding and developing a good working partnership and, inversely, there's absolute horror and endless headaches in having a bad partnership.

Yes, there are people issues to consider for sure when putting together a partnership deal, so the core of any well-structured partnership is a businesslike attitude between the parties involved.

You should always strive to keep the relationship 100% professional. Don't get emotionally involved. Stay objective and focus on the profitability of the deal. On that note, let's talk about a bit 'touchy-feely' concerning finding partners.

Question: Is it advisable to partner on deals with close friends or family members?

This is a very tricky situation and oftentimes, doing this can either make or break the relationship. Here's a checklist I personally use to help me decide whether partnering up with friends or family is an option:

Do Business With Friends And Family Only If:

- They are business savvy and will allow you to remain in control of the deal

- They can bring something essential or critical to the deal such as money, credit, business experience or the like

- You're fairly certain they can maintain a positive, or at least an objective, point of view even when 'trouble' arise based on their past behavior patterns

- You're willing to risk totally losing the relationship if the deal goes bad

If you're considering having a partnership structure for when you do deals, make sure to consult a lawyer to help you structure the partnership properly where everyone is sufficiently protected. And make sure that you and your partner are in total understanding and in absolute agreement on what your respective roles are during the deal, as well as your mutual expectations from one another.

For those of you that are want to learn more about partnering to help grow your real estate investing business, be sure to check out www.FlipAHouseBook.com/resources and look for 'Partnering For Properties' which is a training event I held with a friend of mine that goes in depth into the ins and outs of partnering and how to effectively use them to put together your deals. This site is geared towards those of you looking to seriously pursue partnership deals and make this a critical piece of your financing game plan.

PRIVATE MONEY

Private Money is relationship based lending. It is where regular, everyday, people lend you the capital you need to buy and fix the houses you flip in exchange for a mutually agreed upon fee or interest.

Private money can come from many different sources. It could be a family member, a friend, a business associate or even the guy walking down your street. Practically anyone who loans money to people to buy and fix up a property to flip is a source of private money. These loans can be made from cash reserves or from self-directed IRAs.

There are a lot of great advantages for you and your private money lender and the biggest is that you can structure the terms virtually any way you like as long as your lender is in agreement.

A lot of investors think it is difficult to raise private money, but this couldn't be further from the truth. Realize that in our current economy there is so much volatility in the stock market that many people have decided to pull their money out of the stock market entirely. And what do these people do with their money? Often times, nothing. Herein lies the great opportunity.

Out of all the available funding options for deals, I overwhelmingly prefer using private money. In fact, I finance a majority of my deals, probably about 90%, with private money lenders who are looking for alternative investment opportunities other than the stock market. It's a total win-win scenario for you and your private lender - they have the opportunity to earn a decent rate of return by loaning money that is secured by real estate and you get the opportunity to do deals. Talk about perfection. :-)

Here are some of the typical advantages of using Private Money to fund your flips:

- No Credit Check

- Lower Interest Rates

- No Down Payments

- Reduced Closing Costs

- Cash At Closing

When you use a private lender's cash or IRA funds for your deals, this essentially means:

- Lower Prices

- Fast Closings

Private money lenders will typically have cash or funds available in what is called a 'Self Directed IRA' with a company that acts as the Third Party Administrator to help process their investment to your deal.

Essentially, these private money lenders are allowed to lend their IRA monies (without tax or penalty) to average, everyday people like you and me. In turn, we can use this money to finance our flips.

Perhaps the most appealing aspect of working with private lenders is that you can set the terms to whatever is agreed upon by you and the lender. I always make sure my deals are structured for win-win, which means the lender and I will both be happy with the terms of the deal. If we can't work out an agreement where both us will be happy, then the deal's off and I can move on with the next private lender in my list.

I'm not interested in ever doing a deal where one of the parties is not going to be happy with the terms. I get it, it sounds extremely basic and a bit 'touchy-feely', but I've found that there is no other way to go.

Generally speaking, I will work with private lenders that are looking to receive interest rates in the 8-12% range. However, when the economy worsens, its possible to find investors who are very content receiving interest rates as low as 5%.

Additionally, as you build trust and credibility, you can actually obtain loans without any monthly payments. There are private lenders that will allow the interest to accrue until the property sells. I must stress, though, that this is only a viable option in short-term flip loans. Accruing interest is not recommended to be used for a rental or long-term loan situations that would put you in a negative equity situation as well as placing your lender in an unfavorable lending position as well.

But for your short-term flip deals, just imagine the possibilities of being able to flip houses without making monthly payments on the loan? This can be a definite boost to your monthly cash-flow. This strategy has absolutely helped me catapult my investing business to greater heights when I first learned this strategy.

I hope private lending isn't sounding too complicated, because it is really VERY easy. Just to be sure, let me show a diagram that shows how simple this really is:

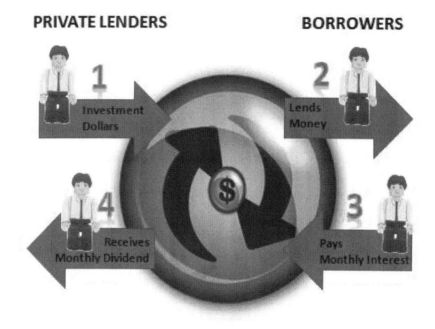

Basically, if you know anyone with cash or retirement capital who is interested in investing with you, you already have a private lender. As soon as you agree with them on the terms, you can begin looking for a deal. When you get a deal under contract, you can present the deal to them and if they are comfortable with it, you can move forward.

If you are using IRA funds, there are guidelines you need to be aware of, so check with your preferred IRA third party administrator and they will be able to assist you and your lender with any questions you may have.

I have worked with several of these companies and I have always had pleasant experiences and smooth transactions.

I've mostly worked with a company called Quest IRA (http://questira.com). They are a nationwide company that began in 1981, formerly called Entrust. I recommend contacting one of these companies and possibly attending some of their free workshops. They often host small events to introduce people to the opportunities of using their self directed IRA's. These free workshops are also a great place to meet investors who may be looking to invest their money with someone just like you.

IMPORTANT

Because I am not an attorney, I do not want to go too deep into this topic here, except to tell you that I only recommend working with people that are already within your own 'network', that is, family, friends, business associates, networking groups, real estate investments and the like. I would never recommend you perform public marketing to find investors.

Performing public marketing to raise money can get you into some big time trouble with the SEC (Securities Exchange Commission). This is why I only seek investments either from people that I have a relationship with or with high net worth individuals.

A High Net Worth individual is defined as someone having investable finances (financial assets not including their primary residence) in excess of US $1 million. Therefore if you're talking with a complete stranger about an investment opportunity that does not have over $1 million in assets, you can easily get yourself into trouble with the SEC and even end up in jail.

Look, I'm not trying to scare anyone here. The bottom line is that the SEC is on your side. They are only there to keep a watchful eye over companies and individuals to make sure that people are not being misled with inaccurate information so that investors can make educated decisions. While large-scale cases of fraud occur from time to time, the SEC, by and large, is there to protect individual investors and it is as simple as that.

I have personally invested time and money to meet with an SEC attorney to make sure I am in compliance. I don't consider this a requirement for all investors seeking to raise private money. Just perform some basic due diligence in your state (SEC laws are different in every state), never make public offerings, only work within your 'network' and high net worth individuals and never mislead anyone and you should be fine.

Once again, I hope the topic of private money lending doesn't seem too overwhelming, because it is actually an EXTREMELY SIMPLE tool to utilize and the ideal way to finance your flips as you progress as a real estate investor. Just make sure that you always perform the proper due diligence so as not to put your lender or yourself in a bad loan position.

The bottom line here is if you exert a little effort to create win-win situations with your private lender, you'll soon find yourself doing unlimited number of deals, unhindered by any funding problems. Always remember to take care of your private lenders and always be protective of their investment and you'll go places.

"For those to whom much is given, much is required"

-Bible (Luke 12:48)

If you're interested in learning more about raising private capital, give the references page a look for the Private Money links at www.FlipAHouseBook.com/resources and another site you may find helpful at www.SimplePrivateMoneySystem.com.

Here is a review of the Key Points to FUNDING:

BANKS

- Not typically a good source of financing, unless you have access to a bank line of credit.

HARD MONEY

- This is a safe source of financing and the most common way for beginning investors to obtain financing for flips, however interest rates and fees are costly

- Use Hard Money in the beginning, but progress to more favorable forms of financing as you progress in your investing career

CASH

- Cash is king, but consider the possible disadvantages of tying up your own cash

PARTNERSHIPS

- Look for mutually beneficial partnerships

- This can be a great option only if you find the right type of partner that you work well with

PRIVATE MONEY

- This is the most advantageous form of financing for flips

- Be sure to follow all SEC guidelines when raising private capital

CHAPTER EIGHT

REHABBING

FLIP FUNDAMENTAL #6 – REHABBING

The Rehab section is probably the most feared aspect of the house flipping process and for good reason, as this is where most investors experience the greatest challenges. However, this doesn't have to be this way for you. You are very fortunate by reading and seeking out education and learning how to use proven systems and processes in your business right from the very beginning. Just heed the advice I'm going to share with you here and you'll do just fine. I promise.

One of the keys to successfully rehabbing a home is to make sure that you've effectively managing and communicating to you the contractors that are going to be performing the work. During this chapter of the book, I'm going to give you a general outline and base of knowledge about designing and managing the rehab process, but if you don't effectively communicate, manage and lead your team, it won't be done properly.

Additionally, before we go any further, let me say that my hope is that no one reading this book is going to out perform any of the rehab work yourself. Unless you are an experienced tradesman and you have the time and desire to do so, I strongly recommend making this promise to yourself. Repeat after me:

"I WILL NOT FIX ANYTHING MYSELF!"

That's right. Put down the paintbrush! Remember, the real goal of this book is to help you quit your job, work less, outsource tasks and enjoy life more. You wouldn't be able to do that when you're neck deep in cement, paint and plaster, right? Take it from me, you cannot accomplish these goals if you are physically working on a rehab yourself. Not to mention, I have seen a lot of investors try the 'do it yourself' route and it inevitably goes terribly wrong, usually for one main reason - THEY DON'T KNOW WHAT THEY'RE DOING!

Please realize this, there are many pitfalls that can occur during this step of flipping a house if you're not using wisdom. Fixing things yourself, if you're not qualified to do so, is the most notorious and common mistake you can commit. Trust me, I know this from experience. :(

When I first began investing, I tried to take on certain aspects of my rehab projects on occasion, and each and every time, I regretted it. So believe me when I say, leave the actual rehab work to the experts. After all you're working on becoming an investor, NOT a handyman. For example, let's say you decide to paint the house yourself instead of hiring someone to paint. Just think of how much time you have lost that could have been used to seek bigger opportunities, such as networking with local wholesalers who can locate your next flip or meeting with private lenders to do more deals. You could even use that time to just do something you enjoy. In the grand scheme of things painting a house is not typically a good use of your time.

Furthermore, you must also consider the time value of your money and the time it delays you from getting your property back on the market. This is a very critical aspect in making your deal profitable. If you are personally performing manual labor on your flip, it is almost certain you will delay the project's completion. Here's a quick review of how you can potentially impact your rehab negatively, and correspondingly, your bottom line by doing the work yourself:

Poor quality - which will result in no one wanting to buy your property when it goes on the market

Delayed Timeline - you will not be able to finish the job faster than if you hire someone to do the work. Often times when people decide to do it themselves, they end up delaying the project for months longer than it should really take. This is a huge profit killer because of the holding costs and the cost of capital.

Prevents you from focusing on building your systems and real estate team - if you want to truly become a successful investor, this is the area where you should be spending your time. Have you ever heard the saying, "I should be working ON my business rather than IN my business?" You really have to be honest with yourself and ask yourself this question: Am I a real, real estate investor or a handyman?

I hope I have made my point clear here. I want to hear stories of great successes from everyone who reads this book, not rehab horror stories. I've seen a lot of new investors come in and experience tremendous success when they do things the *smart* way. Meaning, they find a good contractor and let them handle the rehab or they act only as a project manager for the job.

In a moment we'll look at what, in my humble opinion, are the only 2 feasible options of how to tackle a rehab:

1. Acting as a Project Manager

2. Using a General Contractor

But first, lets discuss the Planning and Design of a Rehab

DESIGNING & PLANNING

After your budget has been established, then you can begin to weigh the factors to decide what you are, and are not going to do during the rehab. In case you are wondering, what you decide what NOT to do is almost just as important as what you decide TO do.

So let me start by just throwing this out there, hopefully without offending any of my 'HGTV Junkies' out there, but here it goes:

"Your personal tastes and likes don't matter."

Your flip needs to be attractive to buyers, not to you. You should define your scope of work by checking out what comparable properties that sold quickly in that market and price range have looked like. For example, if you're in a neighborhood that retails for $100,000, you wouldn't necessarily need to spend the money that you would spend in a $300,000 neighborhood.

The key here is to make your property as nice as possible, or slightly nicer than your competition in the neighborhood and still be able to price it competitively. So, save your HGTV inspirational motives for your own personal home and apply the proven methods that work.

In other words, stick to the basics, which you may have seen on some of the aforementioned endless shows that are on TV these days by pimping up the kitchens and the bathrooms. This is where to spend the money. Of course, be sure the fixtures, countertops, appliances and the like match the comps in your target price range. If the kitchen and bathrooms look clean, sleek and updated, the house will sell faster and for a higher profit.

I will say it again, when planning the updates for the remodel, I strongly recommend you rehab the property to match the COMPS within the neighborhood and possibly add 1 or 2 updated features (Wow Factors) to the property that are 'compelling reasons' for the potential buyers to buy your home.

If you lack an eye for design, one recommendation is to contact local realtors who know that particular neighborhood well, and rely on them to give you some ideas on some of the popular color choices and upgrades that have worked well in that market. You may also consider hiring a designer, but this isn't always cost effective, and many designers go overboard and drive your budgets through the roof. No pun intended.

I've found that if you give a local realtor, you respect and trust and who knows that particular market, an opportunity to gain your listing, they will be very helpful in providing useful guidance along the way.

The key here is to model your rehab to appeal to the largest audience. I typically stick with neutral, earth tone color choices that will appeal to the largest number of potential buyers, even up to 80% of the market if you do it right. You can also get a lot of ideas by looking through magazines, looking online at pictures of other properties that have sold in that particular neighborhood.

Also, be sure to check out the resources page, www.FlipAHouseBook.com/resources, where you can see before and after videos of homes that I have rehabbed for myself and for with some of my clients.

I hope you carve out some time to view the resources page and be sure to check back frequently, as we are working diligently to upload more and more helpful resources and videos to help your investing success.

FLIP TIP: MIMIC COMPS THAT SOLD FAST

Once again, keep focused on the goal of making your home look similar in color combinations, upgrades (granite, tub surrounds, lighting, etc.) to comps that sold fast. If you do, chances are, you will find your flip positioned nicely for a prospective buyer.

Also, keep in mind that you only get one chance to make a first impression. Don't blow your budget on the interior alone, make sure you provide 'curb appeal' as well. You cannot show off all the upgrades done inside of the house if potential buyers are turned off by the outside appearance and its surroundings. They won't even actually make it inside if the exterior is a train wreck.

Now lets discuss the 2 ways of executing getting the work done on your well designed rehab:

PROJECT MANAGER

This is absolutely the best way to learn the rehab process and a great way to learn the true material and labor costs associated with rehabs which is by acting as the Project Manager.

If you don't have the desire to project manage rehabs, it's still not a bad idea to project manage a few, just so you can learn the process and systems involved to successfully complete one.

One reason it is in your best interest to manage a few rehabs is because it will help you speed up the learning curve in determining labor and material costs in your area. Investors find that after they manage a few rehabs, it becomes easier and easier to estimate the cost of repairs for future potential deals.

In order to be a good project manager, you will need to develop a rehab plan that is within the budget of the project and also coordinate everything within a reasonable time-frame. Those are two of the three main rehab goals of any property.

REHAB GOALS

1. BUDGET: Finish under, or close to the set Budget

2. QUALITY: The final product should be to acceptable standards

3. TIME: Finish before or at established time frame.

You need your flip to 'POP' in the end, and we will discuss in a little bit how to do that. There are definitely a lot of 'moving parts' and coordination involved. So, if you can't commit to at least spending an hour or so everyday to manage the rehab, then you may not want to take on this commitment.

GENERAL CONTRACTOR

Look, I could write a whole book on how to work with contractors and how to avoid the many 'pitfalls' that a lot of investors run into by working with contractors. Unfortunately, we're not going to go into that much detail, but suffice to say, the general contractor (GC) is a professional that is critical to your success as a real estate investor.

Any good general contractor can advise on the costs to rehab a property based on the upgrades needed for the property and provide an accurate timeline and of course, they should be capable of carrying out the work with acceptable quality and time-frame.

If you decide to hire a general contractor to facilitate the project to completion, you must make sure they are superb in planning and managing a rehab. After all, that's what you're paying them for. If you do not do an adequate job of screening and verifying the contractors you use, kiss your stress free days goodbye because you'll be in for one heck of a headache. So I'm going to say it one more time for good measure - choose your GC carefully!

It is expected that your GC should have knowledge of all aspects of a rehab to include roof, plumbing, electrical and the entire scope of work. Ideally, you will find a GC company that specializes in working with investors on flip properties. In every large market, there are general contracting companies that have a lot of experience doing complete remodels for investment properties. The most successful real estate investors have learned to outsource this aspect of their business to these types of companies.

Typically, you will have the most enjoyable and successful experience working with contractors, who are licensed and insured and can provide "Turn-Key" rehabs, meaning they can handle every aspect of the project. Once you have contacted several general contractors, you should obtain at least 3 written bids like we discussed before and proceed with the contractor that you feel most comfortable with and believe will give you the best finished product in the shortest amount of time and, of course, for a reasonable cost.

Be careful of selecting the cheapest bid you receive, generally, the safest bet is to select one of the bids that are in the 'middle' rather than the most or least expensive.

CONTRACTOR GUIDELINES

Let's face it, you cannot be at the job site all the time, nor should you even want to. This is where a trustworthy contractor is totally worth the money.

After selecting your contractor, be sure you have a timeline established for the work to be completed and have a penalty fee set-up if the project goes over the timeline for unreasonable delays such as $25 per day for delays that could have been prevented. Both you and the GC can work this out. Also, the agreement should clearly define, in writing, the scope of work, including exactly what is covered and what is not.

It should also be noted that this process of obtaining bids should be done BEFORE you close on the property, so that after you close, you can begin the rehab the very first day you own the property. The old adage, "Time is Money" is especially true when it comes to flipping houses!

However, it is not proper business etiquette to ask contractors to provide an estimate for a property that you do not have a signed contract on. The best advice I can give to you is to obtain the estimates from contractors after you have sign the contract and before the closing date on the property.

When you decide which contractor you are going to hire, its wise to notify them at least a week or two in advance on when work needs to start to give them time to prepare their schedule and crews.

As with any sound business transaction, an established payment schedule needs to be established and agreed upon prior to beginning the job. Just as important, you will need to have a signed contract that establishes some of the key elements, including commencement date, time-frame of completion as well as a detailed scope of what is and what's is not included in their bid. This contract should also include a payment schedule, commonly referred to as a draw schedule.

NEVER PAY A CONTRACTOR IN FULL UP FRONT. You can put a deposit down, generally 10-25% depending on the job and size. Also, when you start the job, ask the GC to keep you updated on the project, but not bug you to death. It is also recommended you check on the job site every few days, at least in the beginning of a new relationship with a contractor. Don't be overzealous about doing this though. Constantly looking over a contractors shoulder isn't such a great idea. Assuming that you did the proper legwork in selecting your contractor, and they are reputable, trustworthy and capable of getting the job done, then, this is the time for you to step back and let them do what you've hired them to do.

At this point all that you really need to do is schedule a few appointed walk-throughs, preferably at the job start, midpoint and final walk-through. Of course, large scale projects may require more on-site visits and walk-throughs.

If you're really lucky, many of the more professional general contractors these days utilize technology to keep you apprised of what is going on. For example, we provide our investor clients at Invest Home Pro with access to cloud based software that our investors can log in and see things like updated photos, work schedules, what items have been completed as well as project documents, plans and signed work agreements. Believe it or not, many of our clients are investors located in different parts of the country and even overseas. This just goes to show that living in the same area as the house you're flipping isn't necessarily true in today's world.

GENERAL CONTRACTOR REVIEW

- **Obtain bids from qualified "Turn-Key" contractors -** Get Referrals from other investors, networking groups & hard money lenders

- Be Specific with the scope of work – What, When, Where & How

- Use written agreements & payment draw schedules - No handshake agreements here. Document it.

- Time **and date of work completion** – Set a 'fair' timeline, but charge penalties if they go over.

Now let's discuss a recommended Rehab flow to occur, whether you're managing the job yourself, or if you've hired a GC:

THE FIVE PHASES OF REHAB

I could probably write an entire book on the actual phases of rehab and every detail that goes into construction and repairs on your average flip property. However, that's not necessary, you will learn many of these things as you go and some other problems or situations, you may NEVER run into. Furthermore, if you've hired a good GC or if you're acting as a Project Manager and you hire good, qualified subs, they will already have this knowledge and experience and you will be able to leverage that to your benefit.

This section is not intended to provide you with a nitty-gritty, nail by nail example of a rehab. In fact, that's not even possible, because every project is different. These 5 Phases are to serve as a general map of the order our company has found to be consistently the most effective flow of construction.

That being said, these 5 Phases aren't set in stone either and every house will vary slightly. Believe me, I know a lot of Rehabbers and general contractors, and they all have their own particular way of doing things, but overall, our game plans are similar with only minor modifications.

So, in an effort to make things easier for you, I have broken down the rehab into 5 Phases that will help you to coordinate your own projects if you are going to take on the role as project manager or monitor progress if you've decided to hire a GC.

If you are going to hire a general contractor, you can use the 5 Phase outline to discuss their strategy for the project and make sure that it is reasonably consistent with what I have provided you here. This is not to say that you should make the general contractor do things exactly this way because that can be unreasonable and can possibly create friction between you. Everyone has their own way of doing things. The main goal is to make sure your project gets done on time, on budget and with acceptable quality to bring in a buyer.

THE 5 PHASES OF REHAB

PHASE 1	PHASE 2	PHASE 3	PHASE 4	PHASE 5
Utilities	Electrical	Drywall	Electrical	Permit
Access	Rough-in	Gutters	Final	Inspections
Permits	Plumbing	Garage Doors	Plumbing	Landscaping
Walk-Thru	Rough-in	Painting	Final	Punch Items
Foundation	HVAC Rough-in	Carpentry	HVAC Final	Trash
Roofing	Windows		Flooring	Removal
Framing	Carpentry		Glass work	Final Cleaning
	Tile		Insulation	Staging
	Granite		Appliances	Photography
	Exterior Work			

HOW THE 5 PHASES FIT INTO YOUR TIMELINE

A good general construction standard is that if a job is not being delayed by weather, permitting, inspections or other issues out of your control such as lack of utilities, then an average of approximately $800 of construction can occur per workday.

Most subcontractors work 5 and sometimes 6 days per week. This is something you should discuss and clearly define with your subcontractors if you're acting as a project manager or your general contractor so that expectations are clear.

Basically though, this comes out to about $4,800 per week and approximately $22,000 per month. Remember, this is for work without delays. This is also, of course, not always exact. However, this should provide you with a good overview of how long any given project should take. And if you're contractors are working weekends and are really being effective without experiencing unforeseen delays, $30,000 to $40,000 of completed construction in a month isn't unheard of.

That being said, when there are 'big ticket' items such as roof, AC, foundation and others, these generally don't delay the timeline at all because they don't affect the overall orchestration of the project coordination unless they require inspections before other work can proceed. So, if your rehab is going to cost $60,000, you can figure it's going to take somewhere between two and a half to three months if all goes according to plan.

Now that you understand how to accurately estimate a time frame, you can apply that time to the 5 Phases of construction. As I mentioned, I've broken down each phase in such a way that they will theoretically take about equal lengths of time. This means if you have a project that is about five weeks long, each phase should equate to about a week. Additionally, if you have a project that is going to take 15 weeks, each phase could last as long as three weeks.

MORE ABOUT EACH PHASE

As I stated before this isn't designed to be a play by play, blow by blow, description of every rehab. I'm not going to misspend your time by describing every construction item in great detail. However, I will briefly touch on what I feel are key aspects of each phase and give you some general tips and tricks to avoid major pitfalls.

PHASE 1

Utilities

I have seen many flips get delayed (even my own!) because someone forgot to turn on the utilities. This is not a good way to start a project and not a way to make your GC or your subs happy. This should have been done BEFORE the rehab begins, and you definitely want to verify someone has them scheduled to be turned on.

Access

You should immediately coordinate access after closing. Figure out where the key is and either go yourself or send someone to change out the exterior locks and put the new keys in a lock box and provide the code only to the general contractor or subcontractors you're using. Having someone go and unlock the house every time a worker needs access is a terrible way to manage a job and surefire way to get totally behind schedule. You can purchase lockboxes from any local hardware store or Online.

Permits

Every city and state has varying laws and codes regarding permits, so we're not going into much detail here. What I will tell you is if you're working with licensed tradesmen, you should rely on their expertise on the permit process as well as the responsibility for them to pull the permits and meet inspectors for inspections. The permitting process can be a substantial drain on your timeline so be sure to factor in some additional hold time onto your project if a heavy permitting process is involved.

Another thing to consider is that if major renovations were done, many times the potential home buyer will want to know if permits were drawn and their status. If you don't have anything to show the homebuyer, they may be scared off from buying the home.

The Walk-Through

This may be the most important step of the entire rehab. On the very first day of the job you or your general contractor should have everyone involved in the project on-site to coordinate not only, individual tasks to be completed, but also organize schedules and time-lines around each other. This means everyone:

- Painters/Carpenters

- Electricians

- Plumbers

- Granite/Countertops

- Flooring installers

- Anyone else who needs to be there.

This initial walk-through is absolutely critical because it gives you a chance to go over the game plan that either you or your general contractor have put together and allows the individual subs to help coordinate and discuss any potential conflicts or issues with the rehab scope of work. It's also a good time for everyone to meet one another, which helps to build the relationships and generate conversations that can lead to better coordination of the project flow. During the initial walk-through you can even actually start some work, like pest control, initial demolition and trash out.

Don't take it personal when you have to make modifications to the plan after conducting this initial walk-through. That's actually one of the purposes of this stage. It is far better to talk to everyone that day and modify the game plan at the start, rather than do so at the middle or end of the project.

Foundation

If foundation work is being done, it is essentially the first item of the project to be done before anything else, for obvious reasons. Sometimes we even start and complete it before the initial walk-through.

When it comes to hiring a foundation company, it is imperative you use a reputable company because you will have to disclose if foundation repair was done when it is time to sell the property. And if foundation work was done, you will want to make sure you ease your buyers concern that the work was done by a reputable company who provides a lifetime warranty.

BEWARE: There are a lot of unprofessional foundation companies around so I recommend you get good references before hiring a foundation company. This doesn't mean that you should not buy a home because it is in need of foundation repair. Some of my best deals have needed foundation work and I was able to get them at really discounted prices because other investors we're scared off from the deal.

Another thing you can consider doing, which is what we routinely do now, is to hire a structural engineer to assess the foundation of your home and provide a repair plan and diagram. They can also do post-foundation repair inspection and certify that the foundation work has been performed to acceptable standards. I've found that this makes the future homebuyer feel much better about the work that was done.

Roofing

If roof work is needed, you should immediately start working on it as soon as the foundation repair is done. This includes replacement or repairs. The main reason for this is because if you wait to perform the roof work, and there are leaks, this could wreak havoc for the painters and create unnecessary work. This is a 'no-brainer' so don't risk doing the roof at any other time than at the beginning of a job. Also, be sure to check the weather forecasts!

The only exception to waiting to perform roof work is if the framing or plumbing (because of new plumbing vents) will affect the roof. Then of course you'll want to do the roof work as soon as those items are accomplished.

Framing

When framing is required, it can begin as soon as the foundation work is complete. For the record, I do not recommend new investors taking on jobs that require building additions, major re-framing or reconfiguring of existing structures. There's plenty of time to tackle such projects as you gain more experience. Keep in mind, when doing additions and major re-framing jobs, it involves a thick permitting process and potentially delays your project for weeks and sometimes even months. This, of course, can drastically increase your holding costs.

PHASE 2

Electrical

If your project only requires basic electrical work that does not require moving or running new wiring it can be done during a later phase. Otherwise, if the scope of work includes moving and adding new electrical installations, it generally means they are going to be cutting sheetrock. Therefore, it needs to be done during this phase.

Plumbing

Same rule applies here as electrical. If rerouting or adding new plumbing is required for your project, then it should be done here. We also make it a habit to replace all shut-off valves, supply lines and hose-bibs throughout on almost every flip we do. We wait until phase four before we install faucets & fixtures.

HVAC

If you're doing a full HVAC system install, it's best to wait until the end of the project, mainly because of theft. However, I always recommend bringing the AC guys out at the beginning of the job to inspect the system and take notes. You can complete the removal and demolition of all old equipment that is going to be replaced later on in the project and install new ductwork and attic equipment at this point as well. I always stress that you should wait to install the exterior condenser until the end of the project to lessen the opportunity of theft.

Landscaping

It's not a bad idea to do at least a cleanup of the landscaping if the yard has been neglected for a long time. I'm not recommending mulch or planting anything at this time, just a cleanup of the area. If nothing else, you can get on the good side of the neighbors. You can finish up the final touches during the last phase of the rehab.

Windows

If you are installing new windows, they do not necessarily have to be installed now, but you want to make sure they are measured and ordered early on. Also, make sure your installer is skilled as to not cause a lot of sheetrock or exterior repairs so you don't waste time and money fixing up their damage.

Carpentry

If existing cabinets and vanities are going to be kept and painted, be sure to get any carpentry repairs completed during this phase so they will be ready for painting. If you are installing new cabinets, you have the option to wait until after the painting is done to install them or install them before.

Quick Tip: Many investors think that just because cabinets are old, they have to be replaced. Contrary to popular new flipper belief, I rarely replace cabinets. If cabinets are old, but just need some minor repairs, you can just make the repairs and paint them. If they are ugly, then you can simply reface or build new doors and replace the hinges, instead of replacing the entire thing. This is a big cost savings idea and I would strongly recommend avoiding replacing the cabinets unless absolutely necessary.

Tile

I see a lot of Rehabbers wait until the end of the project before installing tile. For our company, we consider this is a must to do in the beginning of the project. Be sure you cover it after installing it so it does not have to be redone later. All of other flooring (carpet, wood, laminate, etc.) can wait until later.

If new tubs and showers are to be installed, then make sure they are done around this phase of the project as well. And if you're going to spend the money on ceramic tile surrounds, make sure to spice it up a little with some designs. Once again, remember to 'mimic comps' as discussed earlier.

Granite

I suggest completing the granite install during phase two as well. I know a lot of investors who wait until the end, but its similar to tile install philosophy in that it causes a lot of mess and dust that can interfere with the paint job.

Quick Tip: I've seen many investors try to save money or get too creative using other types of materials for countertops like Silestone, Corian, marble, etc. Those are fine products and I have nothing against them, but I've found that on flips in my area, granite sells better. So, my advice is to stick with a standard countertop that works well in your area and don't get too creative on your countertop choices.

Exterior Work

You should generally begin exterior work while all of the interior Phase 2 work is being done. This is one of the ways you can drastically speed up the time-frame of your rehab project.

Many investors will wait to start on the exterior until all interior work is done. Many times you can have the exterior work done, including painting in a week just when the other trades are finishing up on the interior so the painters can just move inside.

Furthermore, you want to take advantage of good weather when you can.

Unfortunately, as I have personally experienced, if you wait to finish the exterior at the end of project, you may encounter inclement weather. That can sometimes delay your finished project multiple weeks. Trust me, this is not fun.

Phase 2 Miscellaneous Notes

Now is a good time to order appliances if you have a place to keep them. However, if you are having them delivered to the house, you should wait until the end of the project and make sure they are installed the same day they are delivered. As well, if a shower door or glass or any other custom item is going to be needed, now is a good time to get the measurements and get those items ordered.

At this point, a lot of the 'heavy lifting' should be done as we're moving towards the ever important paint job. That's really our main goal with phase 1 and 2, to get the major components complete so that painting can proceed with as little interference as possible.

PHASE 3

Drywall

There is usually at least some sheetrock repair or replacement for most rehabs. Occasionally you will have major work if you have to "gut' the entire house. This is where you would have your workers do the major sheetrock patches or install the sheetrock, tape and float it.

Your rough-in inspections, insulation inspection, and cover inspection MUST already be passed during Phase 2 in order to start this. If they are not, this is where those pesky permits and inspections can cause serious delay and should take almost all of your focus if they have yet to receive a passing inspection.

Gutters

The actual installation of the gutters may not occur here, but you should at least make sure that the order has been placed so that installation can happen sometime soon.

Note: Make sure the color of gutters you've ordered coordinate with your overall paint scheme in order to prevent having to paint the gutters after they are installed. Additionally, as flippers, gutters aren't always a 'must do'. However, if you have drainage issues with a home, you will definitely want to make sure you get these incorporated into the scope of work.

Carpentry (Baseboards/Doors/Crown Molding)

Most likely, you've gotten your carpenter working on any needed cabinet work already. Additionally at this phase, they should start working on all of the doors, baseboards, crown molding and any other carpentry work that is needed.

Quick Tip: One of the most cost-effective 'Wow' Factors you can provide in my opinion is Crown Molding.

Painting

A good paint job is absolutely one of the most critical elements of a well done rehab. Painting should not be taken lightly.

Our company takes pride in our paint jobs, and hires only skilled painters who really know what they are doing. Good painters are really liked skilled artists, and they are among your most valuable team members. I strongly suggest you try to view some of your painters' previous work to ensure you will be provided a quality paint job.

When it comes to painting, not only is choosing the right color important, but equally as critical is picking the right type of paint finish. We generally use a 'Flat' paint for our flip projects. Basically, a flat paint provides the most forgiving and soft finish, as opposed to luster or shininess that eggshell and satin paints provide.

In regards to color, we keep it simple. We've found a couple of schemes that work, so that's what we stick with I'm guessing a few of you would like to know what those colors are, so here ya go:

Beige Scheme

- Walls/Ceilings: Sherwin-Williams, Color 6149 Relaxed Khaki

- Cabinets/Doors/Trim/Crown Molding: Sherwin-Williams, Color 6105 Divine White

Gray Scheme

- Walls/Ceilings: Sherwin-Williams, Color 7030 Anew Gray

- Cabinets/Doors/Trim/Crown Molding: Sherwin-Williams, Color 7014 Eider White

PHASE 4

Electrical (completion)

This means installing light fixtures, plugs, switches and covers. This is also where your electrical permit should receive the final inspection. If you don't pass the first time, do not worry, there is still other work that needs to be completed and your electrician can make any adjustments and get everything re-inspected while the other work is being completed.

Plumbing (completion)

Again, this is the same as electrical above. Faucets and fixtures can now be installed and a final inspection can occur.

HVAC (completion)

This is typically where we would install air registers and similar equipment. Additionally, at this point it's okay to go ahead and set the condenser and call for the final mechanical inspection.

Flooring

Obviously your tile work is already completed and hopefully you took my advice earlier and covered it so it's still in good condition. This portion of flooring is dedicated to all the other options you may be installing in your flip. If you're going to lay carpet, laminate or refinish or install hardwood floors this is the time to do it.

Quick Tip: Keep in mind that after the floor installers are finished, there will be nicks and marks on some of the walls, baseboards and doors/trims. This is bound to happen, so plan on sending your painters back for minor touch-ups after flooring work is done.

Glasswork

Generally plain mirrors are fine and acceptable for most Flips. However if you're looking for a custom touch, you can get mirrors with beveled edges or custom framed mirrors. Most of the mirrors you will need can be purchased at the Home Depot or a local hardware store. However, local glass repair and installation people can be very competitive on pricing. Whichever the case may be, now is the time to get this done.

Quick Tip: many times you will see some grey areas around the corners of the preexisting mirrors in homes you run across. Instead of replacing the entire mirror, you can use a piece of 2" or 3" trim (painted or stained) to go around the mirror. If done properly, it looks great and saves time and money.

Insulation

If your rehab requires new insulation, or if additional insulation needs to be put into the attic, now is a good time to for that item to be done.

Appliances

This is important: measure twice cut once. This same maxim goes for appliances, measure two, or even three times and buy appliances once. There is nothing worse than getting to the end of your project and going to install appliances that are the wrong size.

We install stainless steel appliances in about 99% of our rehabs and I would strongly suggest you do the same. They don't have to be top of the line. A basic starter Stainless Appliance package works for most homes unless you're venturing into the higher price points.

For the most part, the store you ordered your appliances from will handle the installation as well. Remember though, if they take several weeks for delivery, you should order them right at the beginning of the job or as soon as the carpentry work is complete and you have confirmed the sizes and specs you want to be available.

PHASE 5

Permits

This is where it's critical that you make sure you have received a pass on your final inspections for all of your permits. If, for some reason, you have not, then this should now become your main effort and focus as a project manager.

Landscaping

I have a simple philosophy when it comes to landscaping: "Keep it clean and green". Exotic plants and flowers have never been my forte and I've found that you don't have to get too crazy with the landscaping. Many times these houses will have existing bushes and greenery that you can accent with a good mow, edging and some mulch.

Punch lists, final items

I recommend checking the job nearly every day at this point and taking laser beam focus on getting the project 100% complete

Trash Removal

If there is a garage with the house, we always try to contain all trash in it until the end of the project to consolidate the amount of loads and cost. Some investors will pay for the big trailers or dumpsters and leave them at the project. I'd recommend finding someone local that can do haul aways. This is not only a more cost effective approach, but it's simpler as well when you find the right company. They can come and clean out the garage as needed and charge you by the load.

Quick Tip: Look for items such as light fixtures, doors, appliances, etc. that can be sold or given away. Sometimes if there is furniture or other items we think that someone may want, we'll leave it by the street curb on a Friday and most times it will be gone on Monday. This is not only an environmentally friendly approach, but it can also reduce the amount of your trash removal budget.

Final Cleaning

Not a lot to say here, coordination is main thing in terms of getting everything done before the cleaning crew goes so you don't have to send them back for an additional cleaning or wipe down.

Staging/Photography

We'll discuss the benefits of both of these services, but the key here is similar to the cleaning. Just make sure that everything is done so the Stager and Photographer can easily and quickly complete their tasks and you can get your property listed.

Conclusion

Have you heard the saying 'the devil is in the details?' Well this is certainly true when it comes to rehabs and you will likely see it is easier to start a rehab than it is to finish it. Let's face it, there are a lot of 'moving parts' when it comes to rehabbing a house. The key thing here is to build a good rehab team and find a good contractor or fellow investor who can help you out if you get into any situations where you're not sure how to proceed.

Flip Tip: "Common Sense and Good Judgment"

That saying was what I used to read from an old placard on the wall while I was in the Police Academy and it often comes to my mind. This is a fitting saying to apply when going through a rehab because as you will soon see, there will be a lot of decisions that have to be made, so use 'Common Sense and Good Judgment' and you should be just fine.

CHAPTER NINE

FLIPPING THE DEAL

FLIP FUNDAMENTAL # 7 – FLIPPING THE DEAL

Trust me on this, if you take solid action steps and properly follow the flip fundamentals that I've laid out in this book, then you're going to be feeling pretty good about your flip right about now and this last fundamental will be a breeze. However, if you've failed to execute one of the previous Fundamentals successfully, this one can be tricky.

Lets face it, if you grossly over pay for a property or under estimate your rehab budget, then it's hard to make up for those mistakes here. This is just the cold hard truth. Once again, I'm not trying to scare anyone here, but I do want you going into your deals the 'Eye of the Tiger' making sure that you're on top of your game and executing and each step of the process. So lets assume that you've followed the structure and fundamentals in this book and you're getting ready to execute on the final fundamental.

This means that you have prepared your mindset for victory. This means that you've created your own deal flow network and systems to bring deals to you. This means that you've become proficient in using the Flip Formula to analyze your deals. This also means that you've been using the FreeRehabEstimator.com resource to quickly analyze your repairs and you're routinely obtaining quotes from referred contractors when it looks like you're moving forward on a deal. You've also likely been able to acquire the proper financing in order to close on your deals and, lastly, you've become familiarized with the necessary steps and outline needed to orchestrate a rehab, which will be determined based off other comparable sales in the neighborhood. So, if you have the grasp of the previous Six Fundamentals, then you should be setting yourself up for a nice profit on your deal and future deals.

So, yes my friend, you are now at the final Fundamental and it is time to market and Flip that house. Let's talk about some of the MUSTS you need to have in place in order to do accomplish this very last piece of the flipping puzzle.

Like I said, assuming that you have followed the previous fundamentals wisely, there are just a couple of more 'Must Do' things in order to make your deal a successful one:

1. Proper Pricing

2. Professional Photos

Pricing

In order to set your pricing accurately, there are action steps to complete:

• Verify the Comps

• Gauge the Market

• Analyze the Inventory

• Compare your rehab

When it is time to list your property, it's very important that you don't rely on the same comps you used several months ago when you first purchased the property. It's critical to run new comps to see if anything has changed. Many times you'll be pleasantly surprised to see some favorable comps that have closed recently that may help you increase your price significantly. Recently we flipped a house that happened to be in a very upward trending hot market and we listed and sold our property for $50,000 more than we anticipated when we initially purchased it only a few months before. That deal ended up netting us over $100,000, but that certainly would not have happened if we used the same comps when we first purchased the home. So be sure to always run new comps to verify your initial analysis and also to Gauge the market.

When you are analyzing your new set of comps prior to listing your home, you also want to Gauge the Market. This is different than just determining a value and price point. Rather than focusing on price, you want to look at the particular market and sub-market that you're selling in. What trends are going on? Are there more or less houses for sell now than a few months ago? Are prices going up? Or, are sellers reducing their prices? This is where you're going to combine numbers with a little 'gut instinct' to determine your pricing strategy. For example, if we are seeing fewer houses (supply) on the market than previously, we may feel more confident to price our property a little higher than anticipated. However, if we're seeing more properties on the market with longer days on the market, then we may back off pushing the price and actually discount ours slightly in order to generate more showings, which will ultimately lead to an offer.

It's also important to Analyze the Inventory that you are seeing in the market. Sometimes there may be more properties on the market than previously, but perhaps these properties are not even comparable to yours. For example, foreclosures and owner occupied homes that are worn down and in need of massive repairs do not represent true competition to your home, so those types of properties do not gain the same consideration of other comparable properties.

The last thing you'll want to do before settling on your final pricing strategy is to compare your Rehab to the other top dollar comps. Generally, the properties that we flip are the nicest properties that are going to be in market, or comparable to the best. However, there are occasions when other investors or homeowners come in and 'over-rehab' (for lack of a better term) a property to the point that we do not consider or compare our property to theirs. Don't let your ego get disrupted because of this, simply toss that property out of your analysis and focus on more similar properties. Trust me, you'll be in a better position in your business when you are not the guy that is 'over-rehabbing' deals.

One of the critical factors in getting a quick sale is to learn how to price your property right. If you price your property too high initially, you will drastically decrease the amount of traffic of potential buyers. The key to pricing is to get the highest number of qualified potential buyers through the door to view the property. So be sure that you verify the comps, gauge the market, analyze the inventory and compare your rehab before you set your price.

Typically my strategy is to find out what the reasonable top dollar price is THEN price it slightly under that price point (generally only about 1-2% less). This typically means that my home is price equally or slightly less than my competition YET I have a better product. I hope you are seeing the genius of this business model here.

Let me restate and re-emphasize this:

If you price your home equally or slightly less than your competition but your product is better than the competition, who's home do you think will get the most showings?

And who's home to you think will sell quicker?

You got it.

This is why I love the house flipping business model. When executed properly through all Seven Fundamentals right up to this pricing strategy, it's a business model and opportunity that simply doesn't exist in other businesses. Think about it, in what other businesses can you provide a better product than your competition that is actually priced less? I know, it's a beautiful thing isn't it?

That being said, I'm always prepared for the worst with every deal I do. I've been through some rough markets, so I've learned the importance of 'Staying Power' and I've seen investors who've painted themselves into a corner when markets shifted and they ended up not being able to maneuver through some of the challenging times a market presents. That being said, every time I preparing to flip a property, I usually have about 3 price points that are available to buyers. Although, no one is really going to know about options 2 and 3 unless the market absolutely tanks, at least I have some options in case this happens and I will discuss why later.

Here are the 3 price options:

1. List price

2. Investor Price

3. Owner Financing Price

We'll discuss these in just a moment when we discuss Multiple Exit Strategies. But first, lets talk about another critical factor within this final Fundamental.

PHOTOS

Flip Tip: Don't Settle for Bad Photos

I'm going to make this lesson short and sweet. Use a professional photographer that specializes in real estate photos. No exceptions. Got it? Good.

Professional photos typically only cost around $100-150, so this is not a big expense, and therefore there's really not a valid reason to not use the services of a professional photographer. I personally like the wide lens shots, especially on smaller sized properties.

Lets face it, almost everyone who comes to view your property will do so because they saw it somewhere else. This means on the MLS, on a real estate website, on a flyer etc. and all they are judging it off of in any of those venues is pictures, so they better be good. I've seen houses sit on the market for months with poor photos and as soon as the photos were updated they instantly received showings and multiple offers. I know this because this was exactly what happened with my first personal home many, many years ago when I was just started in the flipping business.

My agent had listed our home and it had been sitting on the market for months. Yes, I admit it, I sent my agent the photos that I took from my cell phone and, to say they were not good is an understatement. The fact that our house wasn't selling wasn't really a big deal because we were in no rush to sell it, and we weren't going to discount our price. However, after a few months on the market, my wife and I decided to get serious about it. So, I called a professional Photographer and BOOM, we had a contract in less than 5 days simply from one change in the listing: The Pictures.

If you want to see these actual photos of my house and compare my pictures to the professional photographers, once again, be sure to check out www.FlipAHouseBook.com/resources.

LISTING STRATEGY

In my opinion, there is only one viable way to list a property to sell, and that way is with an agent. Now there are a couple of different options you have with the types of Realtor listings, for example you have the option to go with a full-service/standard listing, or a flat-fee listing. We'll discuss both shortly.

If you decide to list it on your own going the 'FSBO' (For Sale By Owner) method, which I don't recommend, but we'll discuss it because it is an option that I see some investors take. Although, typically regretfully.

The first step to getting your property listed is by finding a good listing agent/realtor. This process should have actually begun prior to starting the rehab, or during the rehab. When it comes to selecting an agent, you basically have the two options I mentioned a moment ago:

- Flat Fee Listing

- Standard or Full-Listing

A **Flat Fee Listing** is a realtor service that will list your property for a flat fee price as low as $99 and this service will post your listing on the MLS (Multiple Listing Service).

The advantage to this option is that when the property sells, you do NOT have to pay the typical 6% of realtor's commissions. You will only have to pay 3% commission to the buyer's agent. In some of the lower end or small starter neighborhoods, this is a great listing strategy, and is often times the preferred listing option as it results in huge savings.

A Standard/Full-Service Listing is done with a realtor that is hired to list your property. This realtor will list and market to your property to sell, in exchange for a commission when it sells. If you go with this option, you will pay a total of 6% commission at closing (3% to the Listing Agent & 3% to the buyers agent).

This option is typically preferred in some of the 'trickier' upper end neighborhoods that are better suited for an agent that has specific knowledge of that specific market. Or, on occasion, in niche markets where it can be difficult to sell houses with only an MLS listing.

For the most part, if you have an ARV of over $300,000, you should consider using a full service listing. It's generally worth it to have someone marketing the property full time, holding open houses on the weekends, and just generally driving traffic to your property.

Of course, if you have your Realtors license you can certainly list your properties yourself if you choose. I've had my license for years, but actually I've used multiple agents for many years to list my properties. Both with flat-fee listings on homes under the $300,000 range typically and with standard listings for the properties over $300,000. Once again, just like I've referenced in other areas of this book, you have to determine where you're 'highest/best' time can be spent. Most likely, you'll find the most successful investors dedicate a majority of their time working to generate deal flow and to raise capital to do more deals. But to each his own. Just keep in mind that if you are spending time listing and marketing your deals, you are taking away time from working on the other areas of your business.

I mentioned earlier in the Deal Flow Fundamental section that I let Realtors know that if they bring me a deal that I like and subsequently buy, I will also let them list it for resale after the property is rehabbed. However, I will often times negotiate for a discounted commission (for example 2% instead of 3% or, if I'm giving them a lot of listings, I might ask for 1.5% after a certain number of listings) or a Flat Fee Listing amount. One agent that we used for many years listed all of our properties at 2%.

When working with your agent, of if you're listing properties on your own, here are some other ideas you may want to consider and test out in order to increase showings to your listings by enticing the Agents:

Offer BTSA's - This stands for 'Bonus to Sellers Agent'. Basically this is where you offer to pay an agent an additional commission if they bring the buyer that ultimately buys your home

iPads - Another incentive to help Agents schedule more showings to your Flips.

Other Bonuses - Other bonuses such as gift cards, flat screen TV's or whatever you can think of can be offered.

Now, lets talk about a 'Do it yourself' listing option that is fairly popular, but not very effective in my opinion and this this For Sale By Owner. Listing a property to sell using the 'For Sal By Owner' method is primarily a way to market the property yourself to prevent paying realtor's commissions. This may be somewhat effective used as a strategy to market your property to Landlords or Investors groups if you are willing to sell at a discount and not in a rush to sell the house quickly. However, this is not necessarily a recommended option to sell homes to retail buyers simply because it does not tap into the #1 source of where buyers are looking and location is the MLS. If your property is not on the MLS, quite simply, your property is not visible to the largest pool of investors. It's really that simple.

I will say this, if you want to put a sign in the yard during the rehab phase and try to find a potential buyer that way before it's time to list, well, I see nothing wrong with that. I've actually sold a few houses that way and I've seen other investors do the same. However, when the house is rehabbed and it's ready to list, for me, my homes will be on the MLS, its that plain and simple.

STAGING

Full staging is not always required, but can really help to sell houses. Actually, most times, simple staging is enough to get the job done and satisfies one of the guiding entrepreneurial principles we have in our office, that is the MED rule.

MED stands for Minimum Effective Dose.

Basically, what this translates to in regards to staging, is typically you don't have to fully stage the home but rather just add some color via towels, pictures, flowers, drapes and miscellaneous knick-knacks, etc. that most staging companies will provide for approx. $400-700, as opposed to a full-service stage which is generally $2,000-3,000.

If you have remodeled your home nicely, you will not typically need to stage a home at all. There are exceptions to this rule of course. For example, there are some upper end neighborhoods that may call for a nice staging service. For the most part, staging is only required to distract buyers from an awkward space to help show them how to utilize it properly.

Lastly, another important key to the flip phase is to make sure the house is being cleaned and the lawn is well maintained during the time the property is on the market (for 'curb appeal').

This may require sending a landscaper to mow the lawn weekly and a cleaning crew to occasionally do a light cleaning, mostly the floors, from the possible buyers foot traffic and dead bugs that routinely/mysteriously appear.

FLIP QUESTION?

FAST NICKELS VS. SLOW DIMES

We all want to hit the big pay day, that's understandable, but let's face it, huge paydays don't happen every time. And if you're a beginner, it rarely happens the first time out.

Remember the Michael Jordan quote from earlier? Let me add another tidbit in case you didn't know: Jordan didn't win a championship until his seventh year in the NBA.

Greatness and major accomplishments often take time my friends, it usually doesn't occur overnight. And most of the time, in order to get to the championship, you've got to take some hits along the path. So, I strongly urge you to not to blow the whole thing up at this point by getting greedy with your asking price.

This is really painful to watch for me, but I see it happen all the time. I urge you to price your property to sell quickly and don't get stuck holding a house that is overpriced. Especially in a buyers' market, that's the last thing you'd want to happen.

A very trusted friend and business partner of mine has done a great job of planting a couple of very wise business adages that I refer to quite often in the business world. The first is "You can't go broke taking a profit" and the other is, "Fast nickels over slow dimes".

Okay, let's ask the somewhat painful, yet unavoidable question at this point:

What if your flip doesn't sell?

Let's just hypothetically suppose for a moment that the worst case scenario happens and your flip doesn't sell. In other words, your flip is unfortunately flopping. Understand right now, that this is always a possibility. Not all your flips will have a happy ending.

So what do I do in such a situation? My attitude about this is clear and concise:

MY DEAL NOT SELLING IS <u>NOT</u> AN OPTION.

I am going to sell my houses one way or another. I believe this and I go out and work on making it a reality. Remember that mindset stuff I talked about in the beginning? I hope you paid attention because I was trying to get across to you what was a most important thing. Even if I share with you a whole slew of quick flipping techniques that are so clear-cut they're practically flip by numbers, if you don't have the "I'll sell my houses one way or another" mindset, you won't last long in this business. So I encourage you to adopt this mindset sooner, rather than later and let's discuss multiple exit strategies:

Sell to Investors

When we go through downswings in the market like we have experienced recently, it becomes a real good opportunity to flip deals to investors. This is an approach a buddy of mine and I perfected during the last downturn. Basically, we began looking for deals in neighborhoods that had good 'Landlord' properties. Then we would purchase and rehab the houses 100% to get them 'Rent Ready' so they could put a tenant in.

Not only that, several times we've discounted the price of a regular flip to landlord investor. Remember, don't get greedy. As long as you make a profit that makes sense, just do it and move on to the next one. We've even had landlord investors buy our flip deals paying full price.

Typically we would leave the homes vacant and would not lease to a tenant to before we had a buyer. It was our experience that it is easier to sell the homes unoccupied, however we would allow a buyer to begin marketing for a tenant after we received a contract and non-refundable earnest money. However, we wouldn't allow their tenant to move in until after the property closed and funded.

In order to sell to investors, you typically have to leave some 'equity on the table'. In other words, you have to give them a good deal even if you don't make as much money as you do selling to retail buyers. The upside though, is you can move these deals fast. This is definitely the 'Fast nickels over slow dimes' approach.

So keep this strategy in mind on the deals that may be a good deal for a landlord

Owner Financing

This is a really nice way to flip houses, especially with the way banks are hoarding all the money and not loaning it out. Basically, you can get a higher asking price than normal but you will be required to carry the financing for a while. I'm not going to dive too deep into this topic in this book, but you don't actually have to 'carry the financing'. You can just sell the note that you created on the sell or wrap your current mortgage.

For example, I just closed on an owner financing deal where I received $12,800 at closing from the buyer of the home and sold the note and made another $3,000.

Things to look for when getting an offer:

Pre-Approval Letter: Make sure the person making an offer on your house actually has the money, or the ability to get the money to purchase it. This is seemingly obvious, but I've seen deals fall through just before closing because the investor didn't ensure that the buyer was creditworthy in the first place.

Short Inspection Period: The shorter the better. You don't want to sell to anyone that needs a 15-day inspection period to have the house microscopically analyzed. Every house has something that's not "perfect" about it. Houses were made and rehabbed by humans. Someone who wants to pick over every square inch of a home is probably not going to end up buying it because they will always find what they are looking for - imperfections and reasons to complain.

Closing Date: Again, the shorter the better. If you have two offers that are the same and one takes 30 days to close and the other takes 60, that's a difference of one entire month's holding costs.

Down Payment: The bigger the better. The size of the down payment matters ad typically shows the strength of the buyer to actually close.

Earnest Money: Usually I like to see 1% of purchase price or more. This means people are serious about the offer and not just "testing the waters". If they aren't serious enough about their offer to back it with some cold hard cash, they're probably not serious about buying the house. You'll be better off marketing for someone who's actually interested in buying.

Inspection Reports: Almost every flip you do is going to have an inspection report on the back end performed by the buyer. So one strategy we employ is to take away a lot of the 'typical' items that inspectors usually cite.

For example, home inspectors usually take close up photos of old crusty shut-off valves, old plugs and switches, ungrounded outlets, exposed wiring in the attic or a lack of insulation. Knowing this, what we do is make sure these 'typical items' are taken cared of and fixed during the rehab phase.

Handling Inspection Reports: We've already covered inspection reports in this book and the same philosophy applies. Not everything is necessary. However, even when you are incredibly diligent in your scope of work and repairs, you might miss something. If something serious comes up from an inspection report, fix it, even if it's not under warranty from your subcontractors or general contractor. This doesn't mean you can't negotiate a little bit though.

You might offer to fix something serious or you might offer to knock the full cost or even part of the cost of the repair off the price of the home and allow the homebuyer to fix it themselves.

For cosmetic issues and non-critical items I almost always negotiate it in one of those manners. If it's a totally unnecessary repair that the buyers are demanding, you have the option of standing firm and not doing it, or politely explaining why it isn't necessary. You can then offer to do it if the buyer pays the complete cost (or the marked up cost) of the repair.

The main thing is, if as a whole, the repair requests from the inspection report aren't totally blowing your profit my hope for you is that you never lose a deal over an inspection report. Simply negotiate what is 'fair and reasonable' in the current situation and work towards getting the deal closed and walking away with the best possible profit scenario while operating honestly and fairly with your buyers.

Conclusion: The main point I want to emphasize for this fundamental goes back to the beginning of this chapter, and if you follow the first Six fundamentals correctly, and utilize the marketing principles you learned during this Fundamental, you will experience success.

Like I said, don't get greedy. Just as my good friend used to say, "You can't go broke taking a profit" and "Fast nickels over slow dimes". Keep that in mind when you are pricing your flips. There's nothing wrong with discounting the price if you are still going to walk away with a profit.

And simply do what works. Utilize the MLS to put your property in front of the greatest number of buyers and keep a few exit strategies in your back pocket when needed, which come in the forms of Owner Financing or selling to Landlord Investors.

THE CLOSING TABLE

Remember to always apply wisdom when completing each step of the process to **FIND, FUND, FIX & FLIP** your deals, as well as all of the 'little stuff' in between and the results will be much more profitable. However, if there is a breakdown with executing any of the Fundamentals, this can cause the deal to end not so favorably. So make up your mind up to NOT let this happen to you.

Envision you have just completed all of the steps to successfully complete your first flip. Believe it and you'll soon realize you just did it.

Here are some other details I would like to note that a standard closing should include:

- Always close at a Title Company

- Always use an attorney to draw up the documents

- Always get Title Insurance (title policy)

- Always order a survey

- Make sure a proper insurance policy is in place

- Never receive checks or cash directly from your lenders. Make sure that funds are wired through/to the title company

CHAPTER TEN

CLOSING THOUGHTS & CASE STUDIES

Sad Fact:

Less than 5% of all people reading this book will take action

I'll be honest. I just made the 5% number up. But I bet it's fairly accurate and it does make me sad that most people will not take action. Don't be a negative statistic. Take Action.

"Life is meant to be lived. So live it."
-Me

I know how you feel. I was scared to death when I bought my first flip deal. But you know what, when you step out, take action and remain committed, it's like God and the universe, fate or whatever you want to call it, all line up and conspire to help you out because you stepped out and acted on faith. At least, that's been my experience.

Even when things haven't worked out the way I planned, I am still able to feel good about myself at the end of the day because I didn't let fear come in and determine my future. Sometimes that's what we have to do in life, that is, simply overcome our FEAR's and take action.

You can educate yourself, and learn and train, but sometimes you have to just step up, get out of your comfort zone and act upon your faith and just freaking do it!

Here is something I didn't share with you earlier:

I lost money on my first flip.

Yep, you read that correctly. I lost money on my first flip, and to be honest, it was extremely painful. Especially because my wife and I were really broke at the time. I didn't tell you this earlier because I didn't want to scare you off. Here's why:

What if I quit flipping houses because I failed the first time?

If I had given up, I certainly would not be writing this book now. Secondly, I'd probably still be working some job that I really didn't enjoy. Last, but not least, did you see all of those closing statements at the beginning of this book? :-)

I learned a lot of very valuable lessons from that first flip failure and I went back to the drawing board and analyzed what I did wrong (basically, I did everything wrong!). But the thought of quitting never lasted too long in my mind, even though the though did show up on occasion. Rather than quitting, I started doing things the right way and then I started making some really nice money. And the rest is, as they say, history.

That's one of the biggest reasons I am writing this book for you now - **so you will know how to do things the right way, the first time.**

Look, I really enjoy flipping houses, starting businesses and making money. I'm not ashamed of that, and am actually proud to confess it. But, I'll be honest, I get so much more satisfaction when new investors make the commitment to jump into real estate investing, study, seek wisdom and apply these principles and achieve success.

Its an incredible feeling to know that I can assist you guys in pursuing a business venture that can provide you with excitement and financial rewards. At the end of the day, what truly makes everything I do worthwhile, is knowing that someone, somewhere is creating their own success story using the Fundamentals I've shared in this book.

Look What Happens When You Don't Give Up...

Success Story: I did my first flip just a couple months after I quit my job. You now know what happened to that first flip - it failed. I failed big time. If my wife and I were on the verge of being broke before we took the deal on, we were practically buried at the bottom of the barrel after that first flop. So yes, we were really scared. But we were determined to move forward.

Before long, a wholesaler brought me a deal that I thought was truly unbelievable. The only thing was, it was clearly out of my 'comfort zone' and I was still dealing with the Demons on the previous deals disaster.

While most investors might have turned their backs on it, I didn't. I took the deal head on. I took a deep breath, and internally challenged myself to at least be open to the idea to try to flip a house again. I plugged in the numbers to the deal formula, checked the comps and calculated my rehab and guess what, the numbers rocked.

So once again, I crossed my fingers, threw caution to the wind, took a leap of faith and signed the contract. A couple of weeks later, I bought the house. Exactly 2 months from the day I bought it - 60 days total - I was at a closing table receiving a check for **$63,886.95**.

You know how that happened?

It happened because I didn't give up. It happened because I didn't let the first failure scare and stop me. It happened because I didn't let fear dictate my fate. Let me ask you this: Under the same circumstances, will you do the same?

CASE STUDIES

I thought it was important to include some actual deals here to show you that you too can begin flipping houses if you take the proper action and follow the steps provided in this book.

I've included some deals that I have flipped recently to show you this is as real as it gets.

In fact, these are 3 deals that I flipped within just a 90-day period, yielded a combined net profit of over $100k.

CASE STUDIES
3 Deals
100k
90 Days

Case Study - Creekbend

Purchase Price - $125,000
Repairs - $67,000
Sales Price - $275,000
Net Profit - $52,642.31

Case Study - Briarbend

Purchase Price - $134,000
Repairs - $48,598
Sales Price - $255,000
Net Profit - $37,275.62

Case Study - Park Rock

Purchase Price - $65,000
Repairs - $29,000
Sales Price - $123,000
Net Profit - $16,611

Keep in mind, these deals are not being shown to impress you. I am sharing these with you so you can understand that

OPPORTUNITIES ABOUND TODAY and you can begin to take advantage of them just by taking that first positive and educated step.

*You can see a full video of "Before and After" pictures of these projects by going to

www.FlipAHouseBook.com/resources

Disclaimer: I'm not telling you to quit your job right away and start flipping houses. Luckily for you, flipping is very easy to do even while working a job. Just set your goals and keep working towards them every day. It's very viable to flip on a part-time basis, while working your job or creating other streams of income. Once you've done some successful flips and you've built enough confidence to take control of your life, you can say goodbye to your job and start working for the best boss in the world - YOURSELF. And if you choose not to quit your job, that's cool to. The important thing here is that you've increased your Real Estate/Financial intelligence and hopefully you've picked up some new skillsets that you're passionate about and will provide additional income for you and your family for years to come.

One strong recommendation I do have for you is to start with small safe deals and then slowly progress to bigger ones as you gain more experience and confidence.

Heck, you can even stick with small safe deals forever and make a fortune out of them. There is nothing wrong with the starter level homes. As a matter of fact, these are the primary focus in my business model. Where I live, these our homes that retail from $100,000 to $300,000. We try not to go to far above or below that price point, but, there are of course exceptions to every rule.

For example, while working a job, you can choose to begin working on small flips that basically make you an extra $10,000 to

$20,000 per deal. The beauty of this is that these kinds of flips are quite easy to do and you could even do 2 to 3 at a time if you wanted to. Remember that adage I shared earlier, "Fast nickels over slow dimes"?

Being a successful entrepreneur and flipper is really about building a long term sustainable business which means being persistent in increasing your education, staying motivated towards your goals, surrounding yourself with like minded people and continuously taking action.

Mindset + Skillset + Environment + Action = Success

Never become emotional over a house. A flip is a business transaction and you should analyze every decision accordingly. If you analyze a deal and the numbers work, DO THE DEAL. If the numbers don't work, then walk away. It should really be as simple as that. There shouldn't be any gray area.

I've seen a lot of investors commit the mistake of being too attached to a flip and it affects their ability to make sound business decisions. Please don't do this.

When you do experience success, be sure to give back. You'll find the more you give, the more you will receive. When you make money on a flip, I strongly encourage you to give a percentage to your church or a charity organization of your choice. Believe me, it will come back to you in ways you can't imagine. Also, share your experiences, education and time to others. As you begin to achieve success, show others your strategies that are working and you will be rewarded. This brings to mind another saying I came across once:

"A candle loses none of it's light by lighting another candle."
-Anonymous

As with any business venture, expect the unexpected. You will certainly encounter something out of whack every now and then. Either you'll end up going a little over budget, or hold the flip a little longer than expected. Expect that there's always something unexpected that could possibly happen.

But that's ok. Don't be rattled. Just stay calm and focus on the situation. Most of the time, the answer will come to you right there and then and you'll immediately find a way to overcome it. In the rare case the answer eludes you far longer than your comfort zone cares for, remember that part of what I shared with you is developing good working relationships with other entrepreneurs. Reach out and ask for assistance from your network. Someone will be around to help you out. Most of the time, all you need to do is ask.

Life Tip

Be tough like Rocky. Pursue Your Passion.

Don't Ever Quit. Don't Ever Give Up. Give Back

In case you haven't noticed, I'm incredibly focused on efficiency and success and I do not like to waste time. Time is more important to me than money. So, that being said, keep this in mind:

"You can always make more money, but can never make more time."

Time is of the essence my friends, so take action TODAY. You have taken the first step by reading this book. Now take the next steps by putting these fundamentals into action.

I want to thank everyone who has invested time into reading this book. I hope the information within has helped encourage you to believe that flipping homes for profit is a definite reality, and empower you to properly apply these fundamentals and take control of your financial security.

I urge you to take the time to check out the www.FlipAHouseBook.com/resources page. I also want to encourage you to further pursue financial and business education by reading as many books as possible that are in line with the direction you are trying go. Relentless reading has been instrumental to my success and I'm pretty sure it'll contribute to yours as well.

I also would like to introduce you to an online training program I have called the F7XFactor.com. This is an online training program that contains over 100 Real Estate training & coaching videos from myself and a few of my team members as we take you through the entire Flipping Fundamentals in video format. We've included some really design features & elements that are geared to help you create success. Including:

- Monthly Group Webinar Coaching

- Private Facebook Forum to ask all of your Real Estate Questions that are answered by myself, some of my staff and other members of the group

- Tons of Real Estate Forms

- Expert Interviews

- Case Studies

- Instant Access to my Simple Private Money System to teach you specifically how to raise private money for your investing business

- And a whole lot more!

Once again, that website is www.F7XFactor.com.

That's www.F7XFactor.com

Moreover, I also encourage everyone who aspires to begin flipping houses for profit, to learn other ways to reinvest the money they earn. I have seen many flippers come and go, and spend their profits on material items and spoils that soon fade away. Commit to a life of continuous learning. Always be consistent with your desire to grow, both personally and financially. Take the time to learn viable avenues to invest in and most importantly, try to give back to the community and strive to make a positive difference in the world.

Once again, I hope this book has enlightened you and made you see that flipping a house CAN be a simple process if you follow the "7 Fundamentals Of A Highly Successful Flip" contained herein.

Remember, these are Fundamentals and this is a system, so when you properly execute each step, your house flipping business can run like a well oiled machine.

Lastly, nothing pleases me more than hearing success stories.

As you progress through your own path to flipping success, if you feel so inclined, please send me an email, Facebook or linked-in message, or a video of your success story so I can share it with others as well. You can become an encouragement and inspiration to others and that's something that all the money in the world won't be able to buy.

I'm looking forward to hearing your success story!

That's all I got. Now get out there and start flippin' 'em deals!

All The Best,

Brant

P.S. If you're interested in taking your the flip game to the next level feel free to contact me on my personal website and schedule a one-on-one coaching session.

You can do so by going here

http://www.BrantPhillips.com/contact-me/

Or, if you're interested in a Licensing Opportunity with Invest Home Pro for your local market, please contact us by going here: http://www.investhomepro.com/about-us

http://www.investhomepro.com/about-us

FREQUENTLY ASKED QUESTIONS

Is it really a good time to invest in real estate?

Regardless of what the media and so-called business and economic experts say, YES, it is a good time to invest in real estate for several reasons: First, people need shelter. There's always someone in the market looking for a house to buy. What's wrong with selling them one? Second, I personally am investing in real estate this very moment and it's been my bread and butter for several years now. If it was really as bad as the 'doomsday mongers' paint it to be, I would already be out of business, right? Third, have you seen the closing statements at the beginning of this book? Go figure. :-)

Do I need to have capital in order to become a real estate investor?

It's one of the most commonly asked questions in this business and the one with the most firm answer. NO. You don't necessarily need to have a big capital in order to invest in real estate. There are ways and methods to get started and go about this business using OPM or Other People's Money. You can read all about it in Chapter 7 of this book.

Do I need a special license or permit to invest in real estate?

You don't need a license to become a real estate investor. This is because you're not really selling a house per se. What you're actually selling is your position in the contract to purchase the house.

What are the actual material things I need to get started in this business?

For the most part, you'll need the following:

- Computer with internet access

- Cell phone (so people can reach you when you're on the road)

- This book (to serve as your guide)

- Camera (to take pictures of houses or deals you come across) Actually, scratch that, see cell phone

- Car and gas money (only if you're actually planning to go around looking for deals)

That's it really.

Where can I find "starter" deals I can "test the water" with?

You can start by doing an online search of houses for sale in your general area. You can just 'Google' it. Newspapers and classified ads can also be a source of deals. If you are a 'people person' you can seek out your local real estate investors association and start networking with them. This is discussed in detail in Chapter 3.

How would I know how much a house is worth?

First off you don't need to know how much the house is worth per se. What you need to know is how much it is worth after it has been repaired (ARV or After Repair Value). This is determined by comparing your deal with similar houses that have recently sold in the area. Basically, if you're looking at a 900 sq. ft. 2 bedroom, 1 bathroom house in your neighborhood, regardless of whether it needs repairs or not, what you need to find out is how much houses with similar specifications have sold in that same area. You can read more about this in Chapter 4.

Are those online valuation software programs really accurate in giving home values?

Online valuation sites such as Zillow.com or Epraiser.com give fair estimates on home values, but that's just what they are - estimates. Though these values are useful when deciding on the fly whether to pursue a deal or not, I wouldn't recommend taking these valuations as holy writ. The safest way to find out home values or ARV is still to base them off comparables that you can get from licensed realtors. More information about this can be read in Chapter 4.

What should I do if the house I want to work with needs some repairs?

If you are planning to sell the house retail, then you would need to repair or rehab the house. However, I wouldn't recommend you do the rehab yourself. My standing suggestion in these types of situations (especially to newbie investors) is to hire a General Contractor to do the rehab for you. You can also serve as Project Manager for the rehab work but this would require at least a little experience. It still would be best to just hire a General Contractor to do the job for you and just sit around and observe how they go about the rehab process so you can learn it. You can go to Chapter 8 of this book for more in depth information.

Can I just flip the house without repairing it?

Yes, you can resell a house without having to repair it. This is called wholesaling. The most common way of going about it is through 'assignment' wherein you assign your contract (the one you signed with the homeowner) to buyer in exchange for a fee (usually around $3,000 to $5,000). It is a quick way to make money in real estate but you're making far less than if you rehabbed the house and sold it retail.

What forms should I use on which deals and how do I fill them out?

Different cities and states have different requisite forms for deals. While it is going to be beneficial for you to learn which contracts to use and how to fill them out, I wouldn't label this as a 'must do'. What I recommend is for you to get someone who knows the ins and outs of your city or state's contract laws to do your contracts for you (I am a licensed realtor myself but I don't write and fill out my contracts. I get someone to do it for me. After all, I'm working as an investor, not a contract filler or something. I want you to have the same mindset.) You can read more about this in Chapter 6.

If I get a house under contract, does it mean I am obligated to buy the house?

If you did your contract right (which is another reason why it is wise to get someone who knows how to do it to draft your contract for you), then it should include an 'Exit Clause' that would allow you to use an 'Option Period'. This means that after you sign the contract with the seller, you have a specific number of days to do your due diligence (i.e., get actual comparable numbers, inspect the house to see if everything has been disclosed etc.). This is the 'Option Period'. If you discover anything about the deal that you believe puts you at a disadvantage (i.e., undisclosed repairs, liens etc.), you can get this to the attention of the seller and have them address it either by doing the necessary repairs or reducing their price. Otherwise, if you and the seller cannot resolve the issue, you can exercise your option to terminate the contract. Again, this is discussed in detail in Chapter 6.

I don't have money to invest. Where can I get funding for my deal?

There are a lot of options for you to consider when it comes to getting your deals funded if you don't have the money for it yourself. You can either go to the bank for a regular loan (not always a good idea for flips right now), go to a hard money lender (a viable option, albeit, you'd have to deal with rather stiff terms) or through private money lenders (my preferred choice as these lenders are the most flexible when it comes to terms). Read Chapter 7 for more information.

Where can I find buyers?

Much like finding sellers and deals, you can find buyers online by posting ads on several websites such as craigslist.com and postlets.com, through newspaper classified ads and by networking with other investors and realtors. Additionally, you can find buyers by posting bandit signs (check on your local bandit sign laws) and even through social media. What I normally do though, is work with realtors to get my deals listed in the MLS. You can find additional information about this in Chapter 9.

What happens if I fail to find a buyer?

Failing to find a buyer is a common occurrence in the real estate investing business. All investors have encountered this situation somewhere along their careers. If this happens, you run the risk of having extra holding costs eat into your projected profit margin. To solve this, you need to not worry about the buyer you lost and concentrate on the next one. My personal mindset about this is: "I'm going to sell my house one way or another. Failing is NOT an option." Remember the chapter on mindset? :-)

What holding costs do I need to worry about if I don't flip my deal in time?

There are different holding costs depending on the deal, the financing you used and even the city and state you're in. However, the most common ones you need to contend with are:

- Taxes (especially if the delay is taking months)

- Interest payments (if you took a loan to finance the deal, regardless whether its from a bank, a hard money lender or a private lender, the longer the deal is unsold, the longer you have to pay interest)

- Listing fees (some realtors charge you by the month to have your deals listed on the MLS)

- Marketing costs (the longer the deal sits unsold, the more you have to spend on marketing to find a buyer)

- Maintenance costs (you'll need to have the house cleaned and maintained every now and then in order to attract buyers)

.